Printing It

Printing It

A Guide to Graphic Techniques for the Impecunious

by Clifford Burke

with Illustrations by Chuck Miller

WINGBOW PRESS : BERKELEY

Wingbow Press
Distributed to the trade by
Book People
2940 Seventh Street
Berkeley, California 94710

Contents

Introduction

The idea for this book was born at San Francisco State College back when a lot of interesting things were happening there: the Experimental College, the Black Students Union, a strike, people getting beat on the head, and so on. Because all those interesting things were happening, people had a lot to say, and for awhile I was the person they came to when the things they had to say needed to be printed.

Well, since nobody had much money, all those people with things to say tried to make do with whatever materials and skills they had around to get something in print. Some of the results of their ingenuity were atrocious, and others were fascinating and appropriate. Printing for a lot of activist students can drive you crazy, and it did, but I remembered some of the ways those students managed to print without any money, and I learned from them the real excitement of the press, the force of it, a thing the nine to five printers seem to have forgotten.

In putting this book together Chuck Miller and I tried to illustrate how it is possible to make pennilessness and some simple skills work as powerfully as lots of dough and snazzy studios. We had some advantages—a good typewriter, lots of space, a little money—but in designing and laying out the book we have used only those techniques that are described. Hopefully the book is an example of the thing itself.

Without losing continuity completely, I have tried to show some design possibilities, such as various chapter openings and initial letters, calligraphic headings as shown in Chapter 7, and ways to treat drawings and photographs. To type the text we used IBM Executive Bold Face #2. We fudged a little in using handset type for italics, and we had the Bibliography set by Monotype. However, they will help you see the relation of typewriter to traditional types. Pages 53 and 54 show justified margins.

While, as they say, all the people who helped on this book are too numerous to mention, I would like to thank the following printers, suppliers, associates, teachers, friends, for their excruciating patience and vast knowledge, their advice and good will.

Reyburn Potter, Griffin Bros. Western, San Francisco
Jack Lee, Somerset Equipment, San Francisco
John Erickson, Treck Photographic, San Francisco
Bob Hill, San Francisco
Bob Meyer, San Francisco
Jim Wehlage, Sadhana Press, Tomales, California
David Belch, San Francisco Public Library
Hal and Ellen Hershey, Palo Alto, California
Adrian Wilson, San Francisco
Jerry Dixon, IBM Corp., San Francisco
My Cranium Press associates: Clea Burke, Diane Burke, Michael Myers, Holbrook Teter, Marilyn Magee, and Bill Bathurst.

Finally, I would like to thank and dedicate this book to John C. Tarr.

1 Printing Processes

The invention of printing and of movable type was the invention of imitation handwriting--one of Peter Schoffer's colophons (Peter Schoffer took over Gutenberg's original press) claims that his printing is so good that you can't tell it from the work of scribes. I'll come back to the business about imitation handwriting in a bit, but for now realize that for almost five hundred years printing went on in the same way as it started; that is, printing by the impression of a piece of paper onto a raised, inked surface. (A typewriter prints in the same way, only the ink, instead of being smeared on the type, is on a ribbon between the type and the paper.) It is true that the machinery of this printing technique had become so highly sophisticated that, had it continued its ascendency, God knows where it would have got to. A completely different form of printing has emerged, however, which is much more intelligent given the needs and possibilities of a technological society. That method is the subject of this book: offset printing.

Offset lithography (or photo offset or planography) is the process of creating a printed image from a flat plate on which an image has been photographically imposed. The plate itself is receptive to water, and the material that is used in creating the image is receptive to oil-base ink.

The inked image is transferred (or offset) onto a rubber-covered roller which then transfers it to the paper. The image is created by exposing the plate through a photographic negative, which hardens a light-sensitive coating on the plate much in the same way as you would create a photographic print. The plate is attached to a cylinder on the press and passes in turn under water rollers that dampen the unexposed areas and then under ink rollers that ink the exposed areas. The paper to be printed passes between the rubber-covered roller (blanket cylinder) and a solid metal impression roller which squeezes the inked image onto the paper. This process is exactly the same for all photo-offset presses. Present-day photo-offset is a refinement of the commercial development of stone lithography at the beginning of the nineteenth century, a ponderous method of reproducing images which were drawn on a special stone with a grease pencil, then dampened, inked, and transferred to the paper.

I mentioned the imitation of handwriting in early printing. The fascinating thing about lithography is that it is not an imitation of handwriting, but the reproduction of handwriting itself. One authority has claimed that, had lithography been made commercially available soon enough, we never would have had movable types and letterpress printing at all! That is overstated, for the really great thing that movable type did, besides making books reproducible, was to make editing and correcting possible. Working on a lithographic stone was no different than writing out a manuscript with all its chance of error. Lithography, however, had the additional limitation that its text had to be written in reverse, since the image was transferred directly to the paper.

So until the middle of this century letterpress printing, with its tons of metal type and its massive, complex equipment, held sway as the chief method of printing. But lithographers had long before figured out that you could put an image on a thin metal sheet instead of a chunk of stone, and by wrapping it around a cylinder get a better impression than from a flat surface. With the development of photographic emulsions around the turn of this century the way was opened for a concept of printing that is rapidly eliminating letterpress and movable type--the method that has lasted for five centuries.

Think of it. Anything you can take a picture of you can print. And you don't have to work in reverse because the image is transferred from the plate to the blanket cylinder and then to the paper. And the plate is a sheet of aluminum that weighs a few ounces. A thousand pages take up the space of ten letterpress forms, and weigh less. It's like magic. The scribes of the fifteenth century are returning in the twentieth, because now calligraphy is no longer an esoteric craft, but a practical and handsome method of producing thousands of books, posters, and broadsides.

Where the revolution toward offset printing really got its start was with small "duplicators," letter size (10 x 15 inch) presses designed to replace the mimeograph machine in offices and small print shops that catered to the needs of small businesses. Almost as small and easy to operate as a mimeograph, the use of these machines has spread into offices, shops, garages and basements throughout the United States. Where once a peace group or a church organization had a mimeograph they now have a Multilith or an A. B. Dick offset press. The offset press in large sizes has also made inroads into even the newspaper business, the most hidebound area of the industry. Small newspaper publishers are switching to web-fed offset presses in increasing numbers, and it won't be long before major dailies will begin to switch over. Already we are seeing mass market paperback books printed by offset rather than letterpress or the common rubber plate method. And, of course, high-quality magazines and textbooks, where full-color illustrations and complicated diagrams are essential, have been using photo offset for some time.

Two other developments are excellent illustrations of the demise of traditional printing and the rise of the new processes. One is the closing of venerable old printing and typographic firms all over the country. Because of the increased costs of space and labor, and the relative slowness of the machinery, even the finest letterpress or letterpress-related operations are finding it impossible to compete. Second, the appearance of "Instant Printing" franchise shops, that offer quick and cheap platemaking facilities combined with a small offset press, has begun to drive out the old-fashioned job printing shop.

What all this means to the amateur printer, to the person using print as a way to communicate whatever political, religious, or social ideas, is that printing is within the immediate reach of anyone with an idea, a pen, and black ink. Formerly you had to put up with the slowness of typesetting and proofreading, the limitations of the types in the shop you dealt with, costly zinc engravings for illustrations, querulous printers. Using the offset technique, even if you don't have your own equipment, gives much more freedom and control to the buyer. The only process that allowed the originator of the material as much freedom was the mimeograph (I will deal with that process shortly). But if the person planning printed material is to have more control over the product he is making, he has then to have some idea (I should say a very clear idea) of how to plan and prepare copy and the original to be photographed.

It seems there is a gap in the kind of training a person can get to learn these skills. While graphic art and design classes teach a person how to make nice things, they give him little idea of the realities of commercial printing such as paper sizes, press limitations, etc. On the other hand, if a person studies printing he is taught how to center his name on a business card in metal type, or how to wash a platen press, and that's even further removed from reality. I hope the following chapters will help fill that gap by stressing realities and being ever practical.

While much of what follows in the rest of the book applies to any press, and really to any printing process since the stress is on preparation, I will concern myself with equipment that can be used in any office, or that might be found in a basement or kitchen. These machines are generally called "duplicators" and include mimeograph machines and small offset presses. I will also include something about small letterpresses here and in Chapter 10.

Offset Duplicator

The offset duplicator prints a plate 10 x 15 inches. There are quite a few models available, and I will talk about them in Chapter 10, but by far the most common is the Multilith 1250. Although I think there are better machines available, the "Multi" has been around for so long (since 1935) and is so common in both commercial and private shops that it makes a good model for discussion, and I will refer to it throughout the book. There are variations on this basic press depending on who makes it, but mostly those variations are in size. For example there is a Multi 1250W which will handle a sheet 11 x 17 inches. There are presses as large as 17 x 22 inches that are still called duplicators, and there is no reason not to consider the use of them if you are setting up equipment. The choice of a press depends on many factors that I will discuss in Chapter 10, and usually you will find that you can make do with what you've got. So we will stick to the basic 10 x 15 inch press as the model.

Platemaking

In offset printing the press is only half the process. The other half, and to my mind the more important half, is the

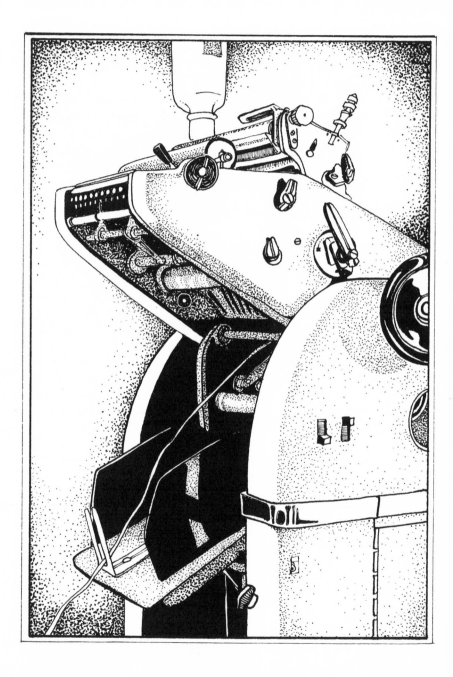

processing of the plate. At one point above I mentioned that anything you can take a picture of you can print. It's not quite as simple as that. Because of the very positive resistance of ink to water and vice versa, an offset press can only print either a completely solid color or no color at all. So the cameras that are used in making negatives for offset printing were developed to resolve as precisely as possible the separation of image from nonimage in the original being photographed. To do this a lens with almost no depth of field is used so that the focus between original and negative is exact (the opposite of a Brownie lens, which will focus from five feet to infinity). No depth of field is necessary because both surfaces are two dimensional. Cameras of this sort are able to enlarge and reduce the size of the original by changing the relationship of the original and the negative to the lens. The negative produced is much like that used for "high contrast" prints that photographers sometimes use for special effects. The negative is then positioned in relation to the plate, and other non-image areas are masked off with opaque paper.

The plate is usually a thin sheet of metal, most commonly aluminum, that has been coated with a photo-sensitive emulsion (much in the same way that paper for making photographic prints is coated). The masked negative is laid over the plate and exposed to a strong light which hardens the image on the plate's emulsion. This process requires the use of a third important piece of equipment. In order to assure that the negative and plate fit tightly together while they are being exposed, a platemaker or exposure frame is used. Ordinarily the plate and negative are laid on a vacuum grid with a piece of heavy glass on top. The vacuum pulls the glass tightly down over the plate and negative and holds them during exposure. Many frames use merely a pressure method. (See Chapter 10.)

After exposure the plate is treated with a developer which washes off the unexposed emulsion and prepares the unexposed parts of the plate to better accept water. Then a lacquer is rubbed over the image area, hardening it and making it more receptive to ink.

This roughly describes the process of offset printing between the original art work, which the rest of this book talks about, and the actual printing, which I am leaving in better hands than my own. (See the bibliography.)

Other Plate Processes

There are two other ways that the original idea gets from the mind to the press, and they should be mentioned here. A specially treated paper has been developed which makes it possible to avoid the camera entirely. These sheets are called "direct image masters," and they work essentially like the old lithographic stones. You can draw a picture on this sheet with a special reproducing pencil, prepare it with a special etching substance which makes the master receptive to water, and print it just like an aluminum plate. More importantly, you can type on these masters with a carbon ribbon typewriter (see Chapter 4) and thereby make an offset printing plate in your office without the aid of the camera. There are drawbacks to this method. Since you are working directly on the master that will be used to print the job, it is a touchy thing to correct if you make a mistake. I would say that it has great possibilities for reproducing drawings: you can sketch out the illustration in a "nonreproducing" pencil, then draw in the final. I will be stressing the photographic technique as the best way to produce plates for printing, but it would be good to keep direct image masters in mind as a useful resource.

The second alternative to the standard negative-plate method still uses a camera to reproduce the copy, but it avoids the negative/vacuum frame/metal plate process and instead transfers the image to a "photo-direct master." There are several variations of this method, but the Itek system and its imitators are the most useful to know about. The Itek system is entirely self-contained. There is a copy board (to hold the original art work), lights, and a lens, just as in an ordinary camera, with equipment for enlarging and reducing by changing the relationship of copy and lens. But instead of being photographed onto a negative, the copy in an Itek is photographed onto a coated paper master that will go directly onto the press. This master material comes in a roll that cuts itself to the right length and processes itself, then shoots the plate out ready to go on the press. Itek is the idea behind the franchise print shops. The process only takes a minute and there are even presses hooked up to the Itek machine in such a way that it puts the plate on the press for you so you don't even have to touch it. I won't say much about automation in the printing business, but I should relate a story about an automated shop a friend of mine saw. He said that during the whole time he was visiting the plant only two truly human functions occurred. The first was when the pressman, who operated the machine from a console filled with push buttons and toggle switches, walked over to the machine, slugged it with a hammer, and walked back to the console. The second was a helper who leaped over the end of the machine, gathered up all the stuff that had come out of the delivery, and threw it in the trash barrel.

The Itek system and its like are a little beyond the reach of most noncommercial printers, and they are really not very flexible. But in setting up any kind of printing shop you should explore the possibilities. You'll find these companies most willing to give you information.

Mimeograph

The great increase in the use of small offset presses does not necessarily eliminate the mimeograph machine, nor does it nullify its usefulness. The mimeograph was invented by Edison in 1889, and is still a cheap and handy resource.

The mimeograph operates by forcing ink through a stencil onto a piece of paper, in exactly the same way a silk

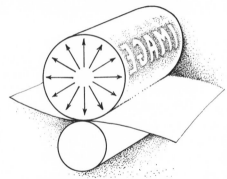

screen or a stenciled paint sign does. The stencil is usually made with a typewriter-- the letters are cut through a waxy film and this film is placed over a cylinder that is covered with an ink-filled pad. Ink is fed to the pad by centrifugal force when the cylinder is rotated in feeding the printed sheets. One variation, the Gestetner, forces ink through a silk screen, then through the stencil, so that the amount of ink that is fed through the screen is controlled. There is a machine, made by almost every company that makes mimeograph equipment, that serves the same purpose as the camera in offset printing. I call it the electronic stencil device because I don't really know what its generic term might be-- each company gives it a different name. Essentially what it does is scan a piece of art work and punch tiny holes in a stencil wherever there is an image. Where once you had to create the stencil for mimeograph by typing or scribing lines in the stencil sheet, now you can use a paste-up in a way similar to offset printing. Since my interest in this book is with the paste-up, I offer the combination of mimeograph and electronic stencil device as a fitting alternative to the offset duplicator. However, I think your time and money would be better spent on offset equipment, especially if you want to do quality work.

If you are using the mimeograph combination I recommend that you stick to strong blacks and whites. Some people have tried halftones (photographs) and shadings on a mimeograph and have made mud of the whole job. While the stencil device may be able to pick up subtle tones, the mimeograph is unable to reproduce them. The most common mimeo machines are the A. B. Dick, the Gestetner, and the Roneo. In many cases a mimeograph can be as expensive as a good used offset duplicator, and you must have a very good typewriter to cut stencils or get the electronic machine, which costs about $1200.00 new. Still, the hand-operated A. B. Dick 90 is a well-made and reliable machine and if you are in a really penniless state you could probably get one for less than a hundred dollars, then borrow or rent a good typewriter and get some decent work out. Many a venerable underground poetry magazine got done in just that way. (I have often thought of writing a social history of the mimeograph in America. One fellow I met described working as a union organizer in the thirties, carrying in the trunk of his car a mimeograph machine and a shotgun.)

Letterpress

The romance that surrounds the world of fine letterpress printing--the interest in and collecting of fine books, and the knowledge and use of beautiful types and handmade papers--is not restricted to the hobbyist or the devotee. Once you take the lure of fine printing there is no alternative but to follow it. For once you start you never get over a love for a page of perfectly handset type bit clean and strong into a sheet of handmade paper, or the brilliant black

of a well-printed wood engraving. And the lure of letter-press printing attracts many printers who are just getting started for many good reasons. Because of the rapid growth of small offset printing that I mentioned above the machinery for letterpress has become quite cheap on the used market. Many beginning printers have had some experience using platen presses and setting type in printing classes in junior high or high school. Finally, if you set out to read about printing in your library, what you will find is material on letterpress, not offset, for all the histories of bookmaking, etc., touch on offset lithography only cursorily, and mention the offset duplicator not at all.

The most common letterpresses in use by small shops or hobby printers are the platen presses. These range in size from 5 x 8 inches up to 17 x 22 inches, and depending on the press, are fed either by hand or automatically. There are also 10 x 15 inch and 12 x 18 inch presses that correspond in size to offset duplicators.

As is the case with small offset shops, the press is only a part of the equipment and supplies; in order to print you will need types, spacing material, a stone for putting forms together, tympan paper and guide pins for the press itself, and so on. I will describe some of what is needed in Chapter 10, along with a comparison of letterpress costs and capabilities with those of offset, but for now it is enough to keep in mind that letterpress printing, even if the type is set by machine, is a slower process than offset, and is not nearly as capable of *reproduction* work as offset. In other words, while it is possible to have a type-high cut made of an illustration, it is not as easy to combine type, a drawing, and maybe some calligraphy all on a page as it is with a camera-ready paste-up for offset.

For this reason, the rest of this book deals with ideas, attitudes, and methods related to designs and paste-ups for offset printing. I hope that the chapters on paper, binding, etc., will be of use to those working with other processes also.

2|Design & Formats

We all have had the experience of being handed a leaflet, and, if we are at all concerned about litter, of stuffing it into our pockets to be discarded later, unread, in the proper receptacle. It is not our lack of interest in the text of the leaflet so much as the inability of the leaflet to interest us in what it has to say that leads to this unfortunate response. Our eyes are constantly attacked with demands for attention from billboards, newspapers, and television. The height of sophistication in these messages, the technical achievements of the various media, and the sheer size of freeway billboards make a humble leaflet for a political campaign look pretty clumsy by comparison. And if that leaflet offers not only inelegance but illegibility as well, it merely contributes to the needless destruction of trees.

On the other hand, leafleting is a time-honored method of transmitting information and one that is much more alive and directly personal than television and billboards. And leaflets can be very effective in changing things in the world. The problem is to make the leaflet as attractive and compelling as its form will allow, a leaflet whose design and content fit snugly with the very involving process of handing it from one person to another.

Most leaflets are done on such a limited budget, and under such pressures for time, that the elaborate designs and expensive reproduction processes necessary for a truly effective leaflet are unavailable. The problems of appropriate and effective design range all the way from printing a leaflet against the war to refurbishing the monthly church bulletin, and include pamphlets of recipes for PTA members, posters for a social event, wedding announcements, newsletters, little books of poetry, school newspapers, and ladies aid bazaar menus.

The problems these many printed pieces share are not printing problems--for printing, the actual working of a job on a press, is really just a mechanical process which, when performed adequately, has nothing to do with the success or failure of any given piece. A leaflet or poster fails because it is not planned or prepared properly, and almost all failures are in planning. One of the most common examples of bad planning, or no planning, is the long and complex flyer printed single spaced, with narrow margins, and on the front and back of the paper. There is nothing to give the eye a break, and even the most dedicated reader soon finds his eye wandering to more pleasant sights. A well-planned alternative would be a folded sheet, giving the reader narrower columns of type to scan, and pages to turn as a relief from reading. The type could be smaller to save space because the mass is not so great, and there could be subheads, as in a newspaper, to break up the gray page. Even if, as in a newspaper, the subheads add nothing to the text, they are still useful as a relief. Planning for this problem would include: an attempt to condense the material by rewriting, testing for the smallest type possible given readability requirements and facilities available, and finding the fold pattern that allows the most text on the sheet of paper. So you see that unless this flyer were printed in a tar pit, the pressman would have nothing to do with the illegibility of flyer A. And flyer B would be readable whether under inked or over inked or heavily thumbed.

The first step in learning to plan printed material is to learn the various forms a proposed job might take, and a good way to go about that is to have in mind a glossary of the standard formats you will be using. Since this book is mostly about the small offset duplicator, the following glossary of terms mentions only formats that will fit those presses (although about the only things the little press can't handle are car cards, art prints, and billboards). Nobody has ever put together a widely recognized set of terms, so every writer on printing gets to define them for himself.

Formats

FLYER (HANDBILL): Handbill is really the more descriptive term, as this is merely a small sheet of paper, unfolded, handed out as an advertisement, etc. But I prefer the word flyer because it suggests the transitory nature of the piece, and hints they are to be dropped from airplanes.

LEAFLET: A folded flyer. In our story of flyer A and flyer B above, flyer B is really a leaflet. Leaflets are more complex and longer than flyers, and they generally contain a text rather than an announcement. A flyer would tell you to vote for Joe; a leaflet would tell you why.

PAMPHLET (BOOKLET): A pamphlet is a bit more complicated than a leaflet. It has several folded sheets, and they are stapled or sewn together through the fold. Magazines, small cookbooks, and small collections of poetry are produced as pamphlets, as are tax returns, forms, and instructions for repairing your Honda.

POSTER: Really a large flyer, intended to be stuck up somewhere (all over) rather than handed out. Sometimes a size in between poster and flyer is used for both. We tend to think of posters as too large to be run on an offset duplicator, but effective posters can be done 10 x 15 inches.

BROADSIDES: Also called a broadsheet, the broadside was a very popular form of mass communication during the eighteenth and nineteenth centuries. Doggerel ballads relating romantic or hair-raising stories were sold by peddlers who carried tall staffs with many crossbars that had the broadsides pinned to them. The form survives today in sheets of poetry and other moral lessons intended to be displayed. The broadside is of no particular size and is unfolded, but is intended to be more permanent than a flyer or a poster.

ANNOUNCEMENTS: My definition of an announcement insists that it be in an envelope; otherwise it would be the same format as a flyer or a leaflet. Announcements are essentially private, and have none of the public flavor of the other forms. Announcements are used for weddings, parties, art gallery openings, and so on. They are usually a folded sheet or card, and traditionally the text is somewhat formal. The size is often squarish, although ready-made announcements come in a wide variety of sizes.

LETTERHEADS: I tinkered with many possible descriptions for this area, which is essentially business printing, and rejected "stationery" as being suggestive of notepaper with violets in the corner. Included here are letterheads, business envelopes, business cards, invoices, order forms, estimate forms, etc., etc. Most of us who get very far into printing will get involved with this kind of work. Business printing can be a tremendous nuisance, but it's an area that can be very satisfying to a designer because it really tests his skill at getting the essence of somebody's work into a few lines of type or a drawing.

I hope that these areas cover, roughly, all the many specific forms of printing you may encounter. You will notice that menus aren't mentioned, but a menu is either a handbill, a leaflet, a broadside, sometimes a poster, or, rarely, a pamphlet. Books are not included because they really go beyond the range of most small offset printers, and bookmaking is adequately taught by some great masters whom I've noted in the bibliography.

Design

Design, in the sense that I use the word, is like the designs you have on your girl or boyfriend--whether insidious or otherwise. I don't intend to use design in the sense of creative art, but in the more mundane sense of planning, John Tarr, the great calligrapher and teacher, says, "If you are building a rabbit hutch you don't just go to the lumberyard and say 'give me enough wood for a rabbit hutch.'" Neither would you put out a poster that contained the text of a complete manifesto which would have to be set in very small type. The designer's primary task is to fit his product as neatly as possible to his purpose. Secondarily, his task is to fit his product and his purpose as neatly as possible to his capabilities. The optimum choice of a person who wants to get printed work done with the least grief is a designer who is also a printer, for he has an intimate knowledge of the impossibilities inherent in any given design scheme. Many frustrating hours have been spent by printers trying to piece together a job that looked OK to the designer when he dreamed up the idea (A production planner in New York calls these guys "paper designers" and says, "They can do anything with a tracing pad, but you can't always print it.")

It seems to me that the best ideas in printing design emerge from responses to limitations: the designer who has countless facilities and a munificent budget at his disposal tends to throw in "effects" for the hell of it--extraneous colors, gimmicky illustrations, exotic types. You have only to look at contemporary printed advertising to see the sometimes disastrous results of the combination of money and art directors. Contrast this to the straightforward work done by many intelligent and creative people with nothing but a typewriter and a Multilith.

John Tarr also said: "You don't print a menu for a meeting of octogenarians in type so small the poor old dears can't read it; you don't print the program for a recital on paper that crackles when you turn the pages." And so on. If his comments were more available much of this book would be unnecessary. What he is saying is that printing is practical first, *then* it is creative, artistic, avant-garde, what have you. It is often forgotten, but notice the printed things that really attract you--you will find that they first of all do what they are supposed to do.

ℨ Camera-ready Copy

If you have a flyer or leaflet to be printed you can take a typed copy of the text along with your idea of what it should look like to a printer and he will do the whole thing for you. He will set the type (which you will proofread), prepare a design for your approval, paste up the text to fit the design, photograph that paste-up, print the job on the color paper you choose and in the color ink you desire, and, if necessary, fold the printed sheets.

Even if you have no skill at printing, everything in the above sequence, except for the actual camera and press work, can be done by yourself, with the acquisition of a minimal amount of equipment and supplies, and knowledge of a few basic techniques. Certainly you are not expected to replace a highly trained typographer setting type on a linotype or monotype machine, nor are you expected to gain the experience of a designer necessary to prepare complex annual reports, books, or catalogs. And if you are one of those to whom the cost of printing is not a serious constraint, then I heartily recommend that you use professionals for all your printing needs as the best way to help maintain the highest possible standards in a field that sorely needs high standards. But this book is for those, such as people in political, religious, and artistic groups, who constantly have the need to get messages out but never have any money. While there is a certain amount of information here for those who want to save money by doing their own printing, the great stress is on saving money by augmenting the work of professional printers. This is best done by learning to prepare your own camera-ready copy for the printer. While many large commercial printing jobs are pieced together after the various elements have been made into negatives, by far the easiest way for a printer to work is from one unified piece that goes into the camera in the same basic form as that which will emerge from the press.

Camera-ready copy for a simple leaflet might look like this: A piece of stiff white board has drawn on it the outline of the sheet size being printed in pale blue pencil (this won't be photographed--see below). Drawn in ink, but outside the area of the sheet, are marks indicating the corners (this is to aid in positioning the negative when making the plate). Within the area of the blue lines are pasted the many elements that make up the job. There may be several large blocks of type, pasted in the proper position to become pages when the leaflet is folded. Above the blocks of type appear headings, perhaps written out by a calligrapher, and still other pieces may contain decorative borders around the blocks of type.

I mentioned in Chapter 1 that the offset camera is designed with very little depth of field and that the subject can be enlarged or reduced when photographed by changing the relationships of the subject, lens, and film. This means that the camera-ready copy must be smooth and flat when shot (photographed). It also means that the camera-ready copy can be larger or smaller than the size it will be when printed. This will be seen as an important technique when we discuss the IBM typewriter which looks much better when slightly reduced.

Another feature of the offset camera that determines the kind of camera-ready original it can photograph is the use of extremely high-contrast material in making the negatives. The negative is either clear or perfectly opaque--there are no gray shaded areas such as you see in negatives of ordinary snapshots. This high contrast insures that the crispness of type and drawings will be maintained, but it also requires that the original be of the same high-contrast quality as the negative is intended to be. While there is a slight bit of leeway, for our purposes we will assume that your camera-ready copy must be made up of good solid blacks on nice clean white paper.

The one sound bit of training that will do most to help you prepare good camera-ready paste-ups is the knowledge of what the offset camera can "see." When I first ventured into letterpress printing and typesetting after working as an offset pressman, one of my jobs was to make reproduction proofs of a book of poetry for an impecunious publisher who came in at odd hours to help set up the type. As I was still unfamiliar with camera techniques and knew nothing of letterpress, whenever a proof came out fuzzy or weak or with rounded, broken, sievelike letters, I said to my customer, "Oh the camera won't see it," assuming in my ignorance that what I didn't want to be noticed would be invisible. The proofs were finished, sent away to be photo-offset, and I sent in my bill. After some weeks I got in the mail, instead of a check, a note saying, in part, "The camera saw it."

For our purposes in this book the rule is *the camera sees anything black on a white ground*. While this rule is variable, it is also absolute. For example, because of their reflective qualities the camera sees pale blue as white, and it sees red as black. It also sees green thumbprints, red wine stains, and flecks of gray cigarette ash. It sees little white specks in the blackest letter, and rough edges on the most carefully made drawing. In offset printing the camera is the taskmaster, and only after this is learned can laying out "black" copy on "white" paper be really money saving and creative.

In describing a camera-ready paste-up I have mentioned pale blue lines and the use of red as black. The use of these two colors will crop up more as we discuss various techniques. The blue pencil is used for all work you don't want photographed, but for whatever reason needs to be put on the paste-up. I've already mentioned the outlining of the area of the job. You might also use it to sketch in a drawing that will go directly on the paste-up, or to show center lines and the position of folds. Also, all notes and instructions concerning the job can be written in blue pencil and will not show up on the job. Red material is generally used in the form of acetates which, while they show up as black to the camera, have an advantage in that you can see through them on the paste-up. In Chapter 5 I will mention ways in which a red material called Rubylith is used to create separations for a second color and to make "windows" for halftones, the other important element in basic camera-ready copy.

Because the offset camera cannot reproduce the shadings of an ordinary photograph (which is just as well, since a press can't print shades of color), it is necessary to create the appearance of shades while actually printing either black or white. This is done by shooting the photograph through an acetate sheet, or "screen," that has scored into its surface a grid of many tiny lines (from 65 to 150 to the inch and sometimes more). The points where these incisions intersect act as tiny prisms to create a pattern of dots. The dots will be large or small depending on the tonal value of various parts of the photograph: smaller dots will print as light areas and larger dots as dark. The graphic work of the artist Roy Lichtenstein illustrates the principle on a large scale, and in newspaper photos where a screen with the fewest number of lines per inch is used, you can see the halftone dot at work. Obviously, the finer the screen the less noticeable the dot pattern, and in the finest work the dots are scarcely visible even under magnification.

The importance of this technique to the person creating his own camera-ready copy is that the process must be done separately from the type, drawings, headings, etc., on the paste-up itself. If the entire paste-up were shot through a

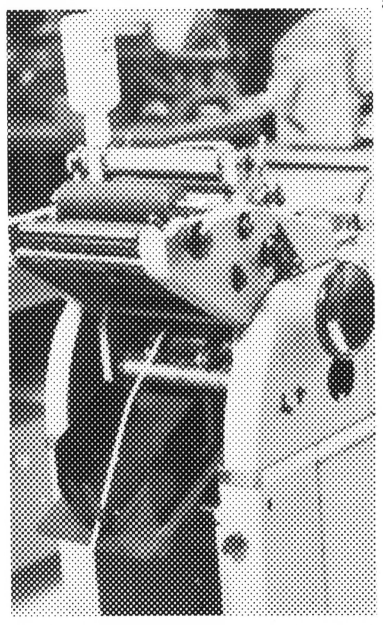

halftone screen the job would be covered with a gray tone, and even the blue lines would take on a certain value and be noticed. In Chapters 5 and 6 I will discuss the various ways of dealing with halftones, but at this point you should keep in mind that a halftone is an extra expense that must be considered when planning any job.

In this chapter I may have implied that if a job is photographed from black and white copy it must therefore be printed as black and white. It must be remembered that, although the camera-ready copy must use black and white in order to photograph properly, once the plate has been made the job can be printed on any color paper using any color ink. For convenience when talking of printing I use the word "black" to mean a solid color and "gray" to mean one that is not solid, whatever the color being printed. It is a common misconception among beginners that the colors of the original, say a painting, can be simply reproduced: that if you draw it with green it comes out green. Later we will discuss the techniques and problems of reproducing full-color illustrations, but in order to avoid a lot of problems and confusion you should stick to the rule of preparing mechanicals of crisp blacks on clean white.

Finally I must mention care and patience. Success or failure in a venture such as this depends as much on attitudes as it does on any innate talents or acquired skills. Many printing jobs done using the techniques described in this book can fail, not because of bad design or bad ideas, but because of haste. A complete novice can do a good job using these methods, but only by remembering that his camera-ready copy will be multiplied hundreds or thousands of times, and that care and patience at the start will insure a handsome finished product.

4|The Paste-up Studio

he tools needed for doing camera-ready paste-ups can be very simple, and may be squeezed into nearly as small a space as is available. All that is absolutely necessary is a smooth surface with a straight edge on the left side, a T square, and a pot of rubber cement. For several years the only working space of this kind I had was a small table 20 x 30 inches. I cut a hole in the top about 13 x 20 inches, and installed a crossbar underneath which held two small light fixtures. A piece of tracing paper was stretched over the hole and a piece of heavy glass put on top, making a light table for working on negatives. (Glazed glass would eliminate the tracing paper.) The glass was clamped down with a piece of "Tru-edge" (described in a local catalog as an "extruded aluminum angle bar for attaching to the edge of drawing boards"), giving it a straight edge for the T square. That table was (and still is) used for every conceivable odd job from tracing art work to cutting paper to hand bookbinding and padding huge stacks of printed sheets. With an IBM typewriter and that table I could do the minimum amount of work needed for designing the layout, pasting up, and for stripping and opaquing negatives for offset printing.

The glass cost about $9.50, the two light fixtures $1.00, a friend gave me what wood I needed, and I found the table. The Tru-edge with clamps cost $4.00.

Drafting Tables & Light Tables

In describing what you will need for your paste-up studio, I am avoiding the problem of limited space, as it's impossible to foresee all the limitations. If you build the equipment yourself you can just about fit a complete studio into a closet.

I have noticed that the central piece of equipment, the layout table or board, has two variants depending on the 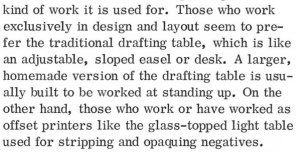 kind of work it is used for. Those who work exclusively in design and layout seem to prefer the traditional drafting table, which is like an adjustable, sloped easel or desk. A larger, homemade version of the drafting table is usually built to be worked at standing up. On the other hand, those who work or have worked as offset printers like the glass-topped light table used for stripping and opaquing negatives.

The main disadvantage with the light table is that it's flat, and several hours of bending over the thing can be backbreaking. I have seen sloped light tables, but while they are fine for working on negatives, which can be taped to the glass, all the miscellaneous pieces of paper in use on a paste-up will keep sliding off. The surface of a drafting table is usually wood or heavy cardboard, and paper tends to stick better to it. Also, light tables are usually limited in size, as a giant piece of glass is both costly and easily broken. The drafting board, especially when custom built for your studio, has the great advantage of being larger, can be equipped with all kinds of storage areas, shelves, etc., and can be built with a height and slope perfectly fitted to your needs. But the drafting table has one drawback; it does not have a glass top, making impossible those operations in which it is necessary to see through the work--as in opaquing neg- atives, tracing, and in a method of correcting typewriter errors that I will explain later. Glass is an ideal surface for cutting with a razor blade or knife, while wood or card- board will eventually become scarred and gouged beyond usefulness.

So, the ideal situation, of course, is to have them both! Since the light table need only be large enough to accommo- date the average size job you will be printing, I would sug- gest a small table like the one I described above. A draft- ing table should be as large and elaborate as possible within the limits of space and money. If you have to choose one or the other, I would consider the light table more generally useful. If you want to buy a small light table similar to the homemade one, a nuArc model 23 x 28 inches costs $120.00 for a floor model, with one that rests on a table top costing slightly less. (These smaller commercial light tables, in- cidentally, have adjustable straight edges on all four sides and are very well built.)

The simplest version of the drafting table, and one that those with no available space might consider, is a simple board, either with a built-in straightedge on the side, or with a built-in T square that runs on parallel pulleys at the sides of the board. The simple board-with-straightedge costs $12.00 for 2 x 3 feet, and could be made out of a piece of plywood and a strip of Tru-edge material for half that. The board with the cable-and-pulley device costs $25.00 for the same size. These boards are used on a desk or table top, and are essentially all you need to do fine paste- ups. Their limitation is merely their portability--by the time you've made them permanent and solid enough to do a lot of work, you've built yourself a drafting table.

Next up the scale of basic equipment is the professional drafting table, built like an easel that raises and lowers and tilts to any angle. These tables range in price from $25.00 for 24 x 31 inches on up into the hundreds of dollars

as they do more and more things only a draftsman would understand. I use one that cost $47.50 for 31 x 42 inches and I chose it because, in a studio that is used for many different kinds of work, it is fairly easy to move around and, frankly, because ever since I started in the printing business, I've wanted a drafting table. They are beautiful and appropriate things, but somewhat costly, especially if you need a big one. A Tru-edge has to be added to make many of these tables usable for paste-ups.

By the time you've got this far into layout tables, you've either got to spend a lot of money or build a table yourself.

The best place to start is with a smooth wood door that costs $10.00, or less if you can find it used. These doors are about the right size both ways and can be cut in half to make two small tables if needed. The working surface is excellent if the door is in good condition. The alternative and the preferable one if you are building to fit a certain space, is to use boards or plywood covered with a piece of heavy chip board. Then you can build to suit the space. The chip board is easy to work on and when it gets scarred from cutting can be replaced. A designer/illustrator friend of mine built a large work area for himself and his partner by cutting a door in half and building a storage area between the halves so they could use one collection of tools and supplies. He built the table using dowels and glue, and the result is a good-looking piece of furniture as well as a custom-made work area. My friend reports he spent under $25.00 for materials. I figure you could spend from $10.00 to $50.00 depending on how fancy you get. The photograph shows something of the construction of this drafting table.

Other Equipment

After you have established your "center" in the layout table and/or light table you have bought or built, the rest of your equipment, except for a typewriter, is a relatively minor expense. Here is a list of equipment, moving from the essential to the desirable, without prejudice, and with alternatives along the way.

T SQUARE: This thing is as necessary as the furniture, so don't try to save pennies when you buy it. A good metal T square of usable length (30 inches) costs $12.50 and anything else (adjustable, wood and plastic, calibrated) is either inadequate or overpriced.

RUBBER CEMENT POTS: These pots allow the brush to be adjusted to the amount of cement in the pot, so that the glue is only on the tip of the brush and not on the shaft where it can drip off onto the paste-up. They cost about $2.25.

SCISSORS: I like good barber's shears, $5.00 to $10.00.

TRIANGLES: You should get a 90 degree triangle at least 12 inches high. Prices range from about $3.50 for plastic triangles to about $13.00 for those made of steel. The steel isn't really necessary.

RULERS AND STRAIGHTEDGES: The printer's rule, calibrated in point sizes, picas, and inches up to 12 inches is a must. Get the best you can, $3.00. Next a 24 or 36 inch aluminum or steel ruler, $3.00 to $8.00. Also useful but certainly not essential is an uncalibrated heavy steel cutting rule 36 inches long, $16.00. A small pocket tape measure is also extremely handy.

RAZOR BLADES, X-ACTO KNIVES, ETC.: These tools wear out quickly and you need a variety around for odd kinds of work. I would say always have industrial razor blades around, and explore the possibilities of X-acto blades in their many forms.

TAPE DISPENSERS: Printers use a lot of different kinds of tape. The easiest to work with is a dispenser that handles several different tapes in the same machine. Prices range from $1.50 for simple ones to $10.00 for the best.

PROPORTIONAL SCALE: Its use is discussed in Chapter 6, costs about $3.00.

PMS COLOR MIXING CHART: See Chapter 7, costs from $5.00 to $7.00.

HAND PAPER CUTTER: This is the slicing cutter used in schools. It is extremely useful but certainly not essential, as paper cutting can be done with a straightedge and razor blade. A useful size cutter, 18 x 18 inches, costs $35.00.

TABLES: For your typewriter, and for space to spread out all the stuff that accumulates around any paste-up job. When planning your paste-up studio you have to remember these areas so that you don't build a layout table capable of handling a giant paste-up and forget to leave space for all the parts that belong to it.

Supplies

RUBBER CEMENT AND THINNER: Be sure to use one-coat cement. It will set solid when burnished, and stays open enough to move around on the layout.

RUBBER CEMENT PICK-UP: This looks like a little stiff sponge and is used for removing rubber cement; invaluable in cleaning up layouts. It can also be used to remove pressure-sensitive types before they are burnished. One can be made by allowing some rubber cement to dry out.

TYPEWRITER CORRECTION FLUID, OR OPAQUE WHITE INK: After much trial, I find opaque white ink is the best all-around stuff to use, because it doesn't tend to thicken and cake as easily as correction fluid. Chuck Miller, the illustrator of this book, likes to use Liquid Paper for drawings because it dries flat and he can draw over it.

TAPES: Masking tape, Scotch or mending, white tape (it won't be picked up by the camera if used on a paste-up), red litho tape (if your work includes stripping offset negatives).

BLUE PENCILS:The great search for the perfect blue pencil continues. It must be hard enough to hold a point, and light enough in color so the camera doesn't photograph it, but capable of making a visible line to work from. It's a puzzle. After trying all I could find I decided that Eagle Verithin sky blue 740 1/2 is the best for the job. Try out several kinds to see which works best for you.

BOARD: For mounting paste-ups. While you can buy commercial illustration board, I find it too expensive. I use smooth white Bristol board bought from a paper company in quantity.

PAPER: For typing proof copy or its equivalent. Professional reproduction proofing paper, called Relyon, is by far the best, but it is expensive and I find that spirit duplicator paper, which is quite smooth, works almost as well. Whatever you use should be smooth so that paper lint does not fuzz the typed characters.

SPRAY FIXATIVE: Sprayed over the finished job, it will keep things from smearing. There are good and not-so-good fixatives. Experiment.

TRACING PADS: By using tracing paper to do rough designs you can avoid wasted time in setting things in the wrong size, etc. It comes in many sizes and weights; pick to suit your needs.

Your best resource for all this, and for discovering new things to use and play with, is a store that deals in artist's and engineer's supplies. Browse, bug them, ask questions. You will find things to work with that I never thought of.

The IBM Typewriter

There are scores of methods for creating the black-on-white artwork for offset printing--they range all the way from an artist's pen to the most complex electronically controlled typesetter that produces finished layouts already in negative form, avoiding the camera completely. The end desired is a clear and legible type that can be produced as cheaply as possible for what you are trying to do. In terms of the kinds of printing work we are dealing with here, it seems to me that for the price and ease of operation the carbon ribbon typewriter is by far the best. If you look carefully at a page typed on an ordinary machine you will notice a distinct fuzziness of type from the pattern of the cloth ribbon. While it is certainly possible to photograph and print from these ribbons, the use of a carbon ribbon, which is exactly like a thin strip of carbon paper on a roll and is used only once, assures that the letters will always be clear and sharp.

Several manufacturers now offer typewriters with carbon ribbons, or carbon ribbon attachments. Availability and cost might recommend their use. But my experience indicates that the IBM machines are the most versatile and reliable. They offer the greatest variety in type styles and machine models, and because of their tremendous popularity offer a lot of choices in used, rebuilt, and rental machines. Here is a case where a corporate giant has made an inadvertent contribution to the workings of the underground.

IBM SELECTRIC: IBM makes two basic kinds of machines, the Selectric and the Executive (I will mention their Composer in Chapter 10), and it is important to consider the difference between the two in order to get the right machine for the kind of work you are doing. The IBM Selectric has the type characters on a rotating ball rather than on the traditional key bars, and is the only real advance in typewriters since they were invented. The Selectric solves the problems of slowness and fragility associated with an overly mechanical key bar system. The type ball is removable and styles and sizes of type can be changed easily, a tremendous resource for the designer of low-cost printing. On the other hand, the Selectric type faces do not have "proportional spacing"-- in other words, they allot equal space for every character in the alphabet, as does an ordinary typewriter. Since traditional "hot" type gives proportional space to the characters according to their natural width (thin for an l and wide for a w, etc.), the Selectric, despite its variety of type faces, cannot imitate the appearance of hot type; printed pieces done with the Selectric have a typewritten appearance. In a well-designed piece this is not a serious limitation, but it must be considered.

IBM EXECUTIVE: The IBM Executive overcomes the limitation of the Selectric spacing while losing its advantage of variability. In the Executive the type characters operate on an ordinary key bar, but the letters are spaced proportionately and a page set by it will approximate a page of hot type, especially if reduced slightly in size. Since this machine is essentially an ordinary typewriter, it only allows for one type face. There are, however, a wide variety of type faces available. It is actually possible to have a second set of key bars and thereby change the type face, but the operation is slow and delicate. The greatest drawback to the Executive, aside from the type limitation, is its fragility. The key bars are for some reason even more delicate than those on an ordinary typewriter, and consequently the characters are prone to bad alignment (the tendency for the letters to be crooked, too high, or too low). While there is no need to worry about this tendency with a good machine under normal conditions, you should always be aware of how the alignment looks on your machine and be willing to spend some money on a service man to realign it if it gets too bad. Also, when buying a rebuilt machine type a sample page and insist that the alignment be accurate before you buy it.

As with the other major item in your studio, the layout table, I would want both a Selectric and an Executive with a good, basic type face. The Executive would be used for setting the text of a piece, and the various faces of the Selectric for inserting italics (to avoid unsightly underlining) and miscellaneous secondary material. Two Executives with differing type faces would be next best. As your budget probably allows for only one typewriter, I would say that an Executive with a good basic type face would give you the best possible overall results. It will mean a little more trouble with secondary matter and italics, but your work in general will have a more professional appearance. A good IBM factory-rebuilt Executive costs $350.00 to $450.00, and rents for $25.00 per month. You can rent a new Executive from IBM for $40.00 per month. If you buy a machine you should explore the cost of a service contract as a way of keeping alignment and other mechanical workings in top shape. Any rented machine should include service in the price.

Display Type

Besides setting the basic text of a printed piece, the other typesetting capability you need is the setting of large type (headings, etc.), generally called display type. The only way to do this kind of setting, unless you can spend money on more equipment, is by the use of any of a variety of commercial transfer lettering such as Art-type, Instantype, or Prestype. Some are letters which are printed on sticky-backed acetate sheets and are cut out and transferred in position to the layout. In the more common pressure lettering method, the letter is placed in position and rubbed, transferring it neatly to the paste-up. (There are instructions for using both these types in the next chapter.) It takes practice and experimentation to become skillful at working with these lettering sheets, but I have seen people become very fast and accurate at it. Neither method seems particularly better than the other and your own preference should dictate. The sheets cost $1.50 to $2.00 each, and naturally you get more letters to a sheet if the type is not too large. The range of type styles is tremendous, and has been adapted from the types of every major manufacturer in the world. A catalog of these types is an important reference book. Stock up on faces you like in several sizes. It is better to have many sizes of only one or two type faces than to acquire a vast miscellany of faces that won't work together.

Pasting Materials

In my list of materials for the studio I mentioned rubber cement and rubber cement pots. There are two other basic methods of making material adhere to paste-ups, neither of which I find as generally useful as rubber cement. Waxing machines are dandy for coating a large proof. The wax stays pliable till burnished and can be lifted and moved, as well as cut. Even if left till the next day it will still be usable. But waxers cost $200.00 and up. And the wax has to be hot or it's useless, meaning occasional maddening delays. Since the proof is carried through the wax on rollers, waxers have a tendency to swallow small proofs, so you still need rubber cement around for tiny work. There is a small waxer, which we are using for part of the work on this book, available for $19.00, called Lectro-Stik. But it is cantankerous.

Spray adhesive has been touted as the answer to the messiness of rubber cement, but my experience has been that, while it's tidy and handy (aerosol can), it doesn't allow you to move the copy after it's down: when it sticks, it's stuck. Wax has a little of the same problem in that the copy won't slide on the layout, but at least wax is easy to lift and reposition. Rubber cement stays soft long enough to let you slide the work in order to line it up on the layout. A can of 3M spray adhesive costs $3.00 and it seems to be the best spray. It's worth trying.

Now that you have all this equipment and all these supplies, and a room to put them in, you have the problem of setting up for convenience and efficiency, and of finding enough light so you don't go blind. Here again careful planning and a willingness to experiment will provide you with a comfortable place to work.

5 The Paste-up

We'll return to the beginning to talk about planning and design in Chapter 9, but at this point let's assume that's all been done and let's follow a hypothetical job through the process of paste-up, and examine the fundamentals of camera-ready copy.

Preparation

Your first step is to cut a piece of paste-up board several inches larger all around than the limits of the job you are printing. If you are pasting up an 8 1/2 x 11 inch sheet, a good size for the paste-up board would be about 12 x 16 inches. Square the board to your drafting table, then using a blue pencil, T square, and triangle, draw the outline of the sheet. If the job is to be folded it's a good idea to draw lines indicating the folds, to show the limits you have to work in. Next, using black ink draw two lines in each corner of the sheet, but outside the actual job area. These lines show up on the negative and aid in positioning the job on the plate. The illustration shows a job set up to fold into thirds, with corner marks in place. This would be one side of a leaflet. You would need another identical layout for the other side.

46

Assume that the type has been set in columns of the right width (or measure) on sheets of the proper paper. These sheets, whether typed, typeset, or done in calligraphy, are your final copy and should be treated with great respect or you risk being done a violence by your typist. In the case of proofs provided by a typographer you usually get two or three copies to play with, but a typewriter yields only one and if you spill wine on it it's your neck.

Next, the other elements of your paste-up will be assembled. You should write or draw repro material (material to be reproduced) directly on the paste-up as little as possible. (There are a lot of exceptions to this, such as informal borders, and you must use your judgement.) Preparing the parts of your paste-up on individual sheets gives you the most latitude for positioning and last minute changes, and a mistake doesn't necessarily foul up the whole job. I find it very useful to lay out all the pieces of a job on a table in roughly their proper positions before transferring them to the actual paste-up. This way you can check sequence and make sure everything will fit, avoiding having to move something that's been firmly cemented down.

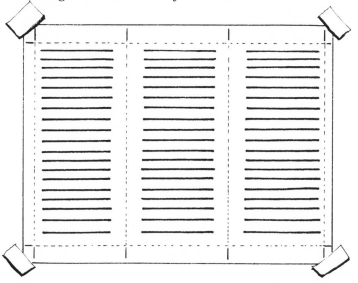

You now have only to transfer the pieces to the paste-up board. Whether or not a design sketch has been prepared showing you how far from the top, the side, etc., the headings and body type are supposed to go, the best way to properly position each element is to place it on the paste-up in its exact position using a ruler to check both the height and side-to-side measurement. When in position make two marks at opposite points with the blue pencil across the edge of the piece being pasted and onto the board. After applying rubber cement the piece is repositioned so that the blue marks line up, and all you have to do is check it with the T square to make sure it is straight. Thus the work proceeds, establishing position, marking, cementing, and then rechecking. No matter how complex the job, the method still works.

Pasting

Now, pasting. I have recommended rubber cement as the best possible stuff to use for paste-up work, and the reason is simply that it allows you to lay the piece of the paste-up in roughly the right place on the paste-up board, and then slide it into its exact position and square it up. This is because the cement stays moist and pliable for some time after it has been applied. Working with rubber cement has only a few drawbacks and cautions, despite the grumblings of many old hands. You should always use a pot with an adjustable brush--this keeps the applicator brush at the right height so that you don't have a cascade of dripping rubber cement falling on the paste-up, on your fingers, in your coffee cup. This one device can improve tremendously the neatness of your work. And you should keep a stack of waste sheets of paper to use as a backing when applying the cement. The proper way to apply rubber cement is to brush it over the entire surface of the piece being pasted--and this means you will get a levee of cement around the piece. By occasionally changing the backing sheet you can avoid getting old sticky cement on the face of the work. Do not use newspapers for this purpose as newspaper ink tends to rub off and can mark the work. If your waste sheets are too small you can buy a ream of newsprint from your paper supplier.

Two other tools for working with rubber cement are important. They are the rubber cement pickup and rubber cement thinner. The rubber cement pickup is like a very stiff piece of sponge rubber and comes in a square wafer shape. With it you can rub off excess cement from your paste-up; the cement tends to bleed out around the edges of the various parts and pick up dirt from unknown places. After the paste-up is finished you can rub off all that excess cement and really tidy up your job. A rubber cement pickup can be made from rubber cement itself by letting a pile of it dry until solid. The solvent in rubber cement is quite volatile, and continued exposure to air will dry it out and make it too stiff to use. Rubber cement thinner can be added to thick cement to bring it back to a usable consistency, but be careful not to make it too thin to stick properly. Experimentation, and examining new jars of cement, will teach you the proper consistency for your use. Thinner, used carefully, will aid you in removing pieces of a paste-up that have been firmly attached. Use a thinner dispenser, which allows you to direct a thin stream of thinner where you want it. By squirting thinner under the stuck piece as you pull it gently away from the paste-up board you can remove it without damage. The thinner dries quickly without staining, and you can remove leftover cement with the pickup.

Finally, it is essential to burnish or rub cemented material in order to insure its staying stuck. When the job is pasted up to your satisfaction, place a piece of tissue paper or clean newsprint over the entire paste-up and rub the whole area with some rounded tool--a soup spoon, folding bone, or the burnisher provided with some Art-type sheets.

Another note here about the camera. While the lights used to illuminate the work being photographed are very strong and positioned so they cast even light over the copy board, it is possible sometimes to get shadows on the copy if pieces

of the paste-up overlap one another, so try to trim everything to avoid this. Illustrations drawn on thick board may
cause the same problem, so if possible have your artist
work on paper about the same thickness as your typewriter
paper.

Typing

I won't presume to teach you how to type, but I've learned
a few tricks that help immensely to make the job easier and
better looking. First, and this applies to any machine you're
using, it is essential that the letters strike the paper evenly,
and hard enough so that the letters are a solid black, but not
so hard they punch through the sheet. Do not use two sheets
of paper when typing; you might even try a thin sheet of acetate behind the paper to give you a harder surface. Most machines have an impression control and you should experiment
with the settings to find the best one. The platen roller can
be replaced with one that is harder if none of the other steps
gives you the quality you want. Some keys may need adjust-
ing to make them strike with the same pressure as their
fellows. I discourage any attempt to adjust or repair IBM
typewriters yourself, especially if you're renting. Get a
serviceman and pay the price. I hate to say this, because
I hate to add to your cost, and it seems that IBM machines
are designed to need frequent service. But after watching a
serviceman realign some key bars you will appreciate how
easy it is to botch the machine.

Your second worry is the typed page itself. The carbon
ribbon, while necessary for crisp copy, tends to smear easily. Each sheet as it is finished should be sprayed with a fixative. It's probably a good idea to spray all work such as
calligraphy as it is finished too, to avoid smearing the ink.

TYPOGRAPHY: It is necessary here to introduce some discussion of typography in order to explain some specific
characteristics of composition so you can use them to your

advantage rather than suffer them. When type is created for
use on a letterpress it's made from some form of lead alloy
cast in matrices of the letters to be printed. This is true
whether the type is set by hand or by machine. Before an image is made from these types they are assembled into the
proper form for the job. Because they are cast from molten
metal, these types have the general name "hot type." The
term "cold type" applies to any method of assembling the
types directly on the sheet, whether by the striking of keys
as a typewriter does, photographing, or drawing the image.
In using cold type composition, because you prepare the image directly, putting down one letter after another, it is impossible to plan for even right margins, or "justified" columns of type. Since hot type is assembled before the image
is made it's a simple matter to justify the lines before making the image. (Justification is accomplished by increasing
or decreasing the space between words to compensate for
lines that are too short or too long.) And since you can make
any number of images from the type you can change and re-
arrange it any way you want at any time. But with cold type
you have only one image--the one you type onto the sheet.
In order to justify the right-hand margin you have to type
the copy once, figure out the adjustment of space to compensate, then retype, making the space adjustments.

Typing the same thing twice is tedious, and errors can be
disastrous, as they give an inaccurate count for compensating. But a justified right-hand margin has been traditionally
considered to be generally more pleasing than one set "ragged." On the other hand you have only to look at a newspaper
to see the lengths to which one sometimes has to go to a-
chieve a justified margin. Quite often you see a line with
only two or three words in it and giant gaps in between them.
Eric Gill, in his great *Essay on Typography,* insists that
even spacing between words is far preferable to justified
margins, and illustrates the idea in the book itself. It is a
beautiful book, even in the reprinted version, and you should
read it.

UNJUSTIFIED MARGINS: The whole question seems to me to rest on a notion I expressed earlier, that of the advantage of limitations. If it takes twice as long (or longer) to set justified copy on a typewriter, then you can assume that the machine can't set justified copy and you can learn to design your printed work to incorporate ragged columns. And let me say while I'm at it that you can't type any old thing and call it a column of type. Great care should be taken to see that the right margin is pleasing in its raggedness: lines should never be excessively short or long, and you should use hyphenation to insure evenness. However, more than three hyphens on consecutive line endings look unsightly. Occasionally, paragraphs may have to be retyped to make the lines look better. I suggest you examine as many books, magazines, etc., as possible that use an unjustified format, in order to get ideas on column widths, size of type, and position on the page. An idea for informal work that I saw recently uses, in effect, an unjustified margin on *both* sides. You achieve this by indenting every other line the equivalent of three or four characters on the left, and maintaining the ragged margin on the right.

In unjustified work your right hand margin will run four, sometimes five, characters long or short of an average which you will call your column width. To achieve this, first determine the column width of your job, taking into consideration that some lines will run slightly over (don't run these longer lines off the edge of the sheet). Then set the left margin on your typewriter, measure your column width, and with a blue pencil draw a line down the length of the sheet you are typing on. Do this for every sheet needed for the job, and you will always be able to see how the lines you are typing relate to the average margin. An easy way to draw the line is to hold the pencil against the paper at the proper place, then roll the sheet through the typewriter, keeping the pencil steady.

JUSTIFIED MARGINS: Some of the more advanced equipment we will talk about later have devices built into them to automatically determine how much space you have to add or subtract in a line to make it justify. But the IBM Executive has no such device, and you have to stay pretty much on your toes to avoid excessive retyping. You should study the Exec instruction manual carefully. I developed my method for justification after an eleventh hour discovery that a typist I had hired didn't know how to do it. It varies only slightly from the official IBM method, but those variants really help when you're besotted or befuddled.

It is as important to get the first copy right as the second repro copy. But since the first one is your planning copy and will not be photographed you can write on it, type over mistakes, etc. What you are doing when you type the rough is spacing, so if the text is wrong the spacing will be wrong. If you see a typographical error (typo) while making the rough, go back to the beginning of the word and retype it correctly; don't mind that you can't read what it says.

The IBM Executive proportional spacing system gives individual characters the amount of space they deserve, based on a scale of five units. Capital W, M, and so on are five units wide, while lower case i, l and other narrow letters are two units in width. Other characters are proportioned accordingly. One unit of space is too narrow for any letter; it is used for spacing purposes only. On the Exec there are two space bars: one puts three units of space between words and the other puts in two. The back space key backs up one unit, and in order to eliminate a three-unit word space you have to hit the back spacer three times. There is a gun sight guide that lines up with the beginning of the letter about to be typed so you can easily find your place. These three elements are the working parts you need to know when justifying copy.

First, determine your measure, as for unjustified work, only this time use a hard-lead pencil, well-sharpened, to draw the guide line. Next, type your first line of copy, putting a three-unit space between words. When you reach the guide line, the last word that you can fit in will usually be slightly longer or shorter than the proper measure. Let us say the lower case e is to the right of the guide line. In your instruction book for the machine is a chart showing the number of units for each character, and let us assume that e is three units wide. In order to make that e justify you must take out three units of space from the line you just typed. To do this, at three places in the line you will insert a two-unit word space instead of the usual three-unit one. Now let us assume that the last word of a line runs a bit short of the measure. What standard practice says is that you fill out the line to your guide using an uncommon two-unit letter, usually j. The number of j's multiplied by two will be the number of units at various word spaces to justify.

You can see from the above how a typo can foul you up by indicating the wrong space, and why it's important to use a sharp, hard pencil to draw the guide line, so that there is no confusion as to whether a letter is on or over the line. For sometimes the last letter will end dead center on the guide line, and you have to use your head to decide how many units to subtract. Simple typos that aren't seen at once can often be corrected just by compensating for the difference in units. If you typed a two-unit letter when you wanted a three, you can make it fit by subtracting or adding one space when retyping. Also remember that the number of spaces you can subtract in a line is determined by the number of word spaces available, so use a hyphen rather than let a line run so many units over that you don't have room to compensate. A line that is too short is just as bad, since very wide word spaces are unsightly.

In the preparation of the rough copy for justification I differ slightly from the official IBM method. IBM suggests when reaching the end of a given line that you indicate +3 or −2, the number of units long or short out in the margin, assuming that when you retype you will check the right-hand margin to determine how to type the line. However, I find the most common error in justified typing is that the typist does *not* check the instructions until he or she has worked so far into the line that there aren't enough places left to compensate. This is not just carelessness; the typewriter's construction urges you to resume typing as soon as the carriage is returned. It also seems inefficient to stop at the end of each line to consult the instruction book in order to refresh your memory as to the number of characters in an m, and then write it on the sheet.

As I said, the way I do it is intended for those who are up past bedtime. Instead of counting units at every line, type the first copy with an eye to good hyphenation and accuracy, avoiding excess characters at the end. Then go back (or a second person can do it while you proceed) and figure the compensation, and instead of an instruction, mark with a red pencil *each place* where a space should be added or removed, in every line. The typist then has only to follow the marks as they come up, and can concentrate on accuracy. A simple code will suffice. I use an inverted v to indicate additional space, and a slash to indicate less. By this method you can keep an eye on the appearance of the entire page, and spread out your compensations so that the page looks even and well balanced. I stress this because you are not able to adjust all the word spaces in a line as you are with hot type composition. If you have nine word spaces to a line and only five units to take up, the spacing is bound to be uneven. The solution is to look for places where more or less space will go unnoticed, such as after a punctuation mark and/or before a capital letter. Two vertical letters look closer together than two round ones, so add space between the verticals and remove it from between the round ones.

TYPEWRITER CORRECTIONS: Among the most common substances used for correcting mistakes in typing done for reproduction are opaque whites which you paint over the offending word, or white typing sheets which in effect lay down a white carbon ribbon over the typo. I have no objection to your trying these methods, but I have never liked them. Kept properly thinned Liquid Paper works pretty well for correcting single-letter mistakes that you catch while typing. But a major correction never really looks right. The only truly satisfactory way to make a correction is to type it separately and paste it into the copy, thereby maintaining as much as possible the pristine condition of the original. While you can paste the correction onto the original, that involves the risk of it falling off. The best method I have found is to cut it right into the original and tape it from the back. For this you need a light table.

If you type on a sheet twice as wide as you need for your column, you can type the corrections beside the lines they belong to, making it simple to collate them. Those lines in which you catch the error at once should be typed over from the beginning of the error correctly, as in rough copy for justification. This keeps the spacing correct. Then type the correction next to the line. To insert the correction, cut the new line out leaving plenty of space around it. On the light table the correct line is superimposed exactly on the incorrect. Holding the two down firmly, and using a sharp razor blade or knife, cut closely around the correction (avoiding neighboring type) and through the original. Taping the original to the light table keeps it from sliding about while you are cutting. The correction will fit exactly in the hole left in the copy, and the two are attached with scotch or mending tape at the back of the sheet. This technique takes some practice. The same technique applies to any correction if allowance is made for differences in spacing. Since the correction fits exactly where the error was, there is no need to check for square, the piece can't fall off, and it can't slide out of line. The light table is handy for corrections even if you don't cut them in, since the idea of superimposing the correction exactly on the original still applies.

Transfer Lettering

There are still some brands of transfer lettering around

which are printed on acetate with a sticky back, and which
are cut out from the master sheet and transferred to the
paste-up. But the great bulk of all transfer lettering is printed on clear sheets of either acetate or polyethylene and then
waxed. This wax adhesive allows you to rub the letter right
onto the paste-up, after it has been positioned, by pulling
the ink away from the clear sheet and adhering it to the layout.

The Art-type lettering, the ones you cut out and transfer,
seem to be much better printed than the rub-on kind, so you
consistently get a much better quality of type. But the time-
saving advantage of the rub-on letters makes them work out
better in the long run. To use Art-type draw a base line with
a sharp, hard pencil on a sheet separate from your paste-
up. Tape the sheet to your layout board so it won't move a-
round. Art-type has printed at the base of each letter a line
that shows not only vertical alignment but the horizontal relationship of the letters as well. In theory, if you place the
base lines end to end the letters will be in their proper positions. This is only theory, and you should rely on visual
spacing as well to get an adequate job. It is a good idea to
cut out all the letters at once and lay them out in order on a
piece of layout board. Then you can proofread before final
positioning and avoid tedious resetting. Cut out each letter
lightly with a sharp razor blade, making sure you include
the base line, and lift it carefully from the backing sheet.
These letters have a maddening tendency to tear. Cut as
close as possible to the sides of the letters to avoid over-
lapping the acetate when lining them up (if you have to move
one you don't want to move the others). Don't press anything down until the entire word or line is finished. When
complete and correct burnish as with a paste-up. Then cut
the base line away from the type and the piece is ready to
be pasted into position.

The transfer letters that rub on are much easier to line
up and position. While they usually don't have any guide for
positioning in relation to each other, it is easier to move

them into position visually since they don't stick like Arttype. The technique is simple. Draw the same clean line on a piece of paper and tape it to your layout table. Take extra care in positioning and squaring, as what is rubbed onto the paste-up can't be moved around. A wrong letter can be removed by rubbing it with a rubber cement pickup. When complete, burnish well (there is a small burnisher available especially for use with transfer lettering) and spray with fixative. Almost any tool can be used to transfer the letters; the commercial burnisher works well. Some use the point of a ball pen, and I have found that the rounded caps on certain cheap ballpoints are perfect. Experiment. The tool should be small enough for fine work, yet not have a sharp point. The trick is to transfer the entire letter (it drives you crazy to lift the lettering sheet and see that you've chopped off the tail of a y) and yet not rub off parts of the adjacent letters. It's probably wise to avoid types with fine hair lines; they just never seem to transfer well. Be sure to work on a hard surface so as not to gouge or stretch the plastic sheet because this will make the letter transfer badly. And do not allow the sheet to slip at all while you are rubbing, as this will cause the letter to crack.

The technique is simple, but the practice can be filled with headaches and frustrations. The greatest obstacle is the recent proliferation of this method of typesetting. The result of that great increase in production is that the quality in general has gone down, and is at best, undependable. Alignment was the first factor to suffer, and you can find on some brands base lines that ramble all over the sheet, demanding grueling attention to produce adequate work. Even more important is the fact that many lettering sheets are just badly printed; thin strokes disappear, and edges are so rough they might as well be inked by hand. This happens because lettering sheets are printed by silk screen from reproduction proofs of existing type. The photographic silk screen process is not the best for fine work, and poor photography is sure to show up. The worst offense is an inability

to make the letters transfer consistently well. They crack
and peel and chunks pull away, and the salesman will tell
you the shop is too hot or too cold, or your hands are clam-
my, but it just isn't true. The fact is that if the wax adhesive is too thick or too thin the letters may not transfer,
and a sheet that is too old can cause trouble. When I was
setting up the trial pages for this book I spent a whole morning trying to set the words "Equipping the Paste-up Studio"
in some uncial type. After trying a half-dozen rubbing tools,
heating, cooling and incantations, I switched to a different
type from the same company. Presto. It transferred like
the instructions said it should.

Don't despair. If you search for the brands that are well
printed, rejecting any that are excessively crooked, and return those sheets that will not transfer properly, insisting
on your money back, eventually the industry will shape up,
and meanwhile you don't have to struggle with the impossible. These transfer types are such a tremendous resource
that it's worth a certain amount of patience in dealing with
their purveyors. Where else could you set up five words in
72 point Caslon for $1.50 to $2.00? Where else could you
get any small proof for that price, any time, and set exactly as your crazy ideas may dictate? I have tested many
brands while preparing this book and found that Spectype,
from American Type Founders, is of the best quality printing and transferring. But the styles of Spectype are severely
limited. Prestype is the best all around, with many type
styles and generally good quality manufacture.

Illustrations

As we will see in the next chapter, most forms of illustrating your work are expensive. But ordinary line drawings,
since they can be shot along with the rest of the paste-up,
are cheap, and can give, when done in the right spirit, exactly the right feeling or tone to a job that might not otherwise come off. And drawings are the form of illustration

for modern mass reproduction in the way that wood cuts
and engravings were for early printing. With drawings you
can reflect precisely the weight of whatever typographic resource you are using. The proper balance of headings, body
type, drawings, and perhaps color, can make a printed
page appeal to the reader in a way as lively and immediate
as any medium. Drawings fit the informality of typewritten
copy. The technical resources are virtually endless, and
even an amateur can produce usable illustrations with cour-
age and a lot of whiting out. On pages 38 and 121 I have tried
my hand with passable results. You can trace photos using
a pen to imitate halftone reproduction. There are not many
rules for line illustrations. The blacks should be solid and
you must avoid washes, the gray effect similar to water-
color, because in order to make it gray you have to shoot
the drawing as a halftone. Shaded effects can be achieved
by cross-hatching lines or by making dot patterns with the
pen. Mistakes can be painted out, and for this Chuck Miller
says that Liquid Paper, the stuff sold as a correction paint-
out for typing (for which I do not recommend it) is ideal for
correcting mistakes in drawings because it dries flat and
you can draw right over it. You are on your own in finding
whites for any purpose, but remember, all of them are sus-
pensions of white pigment in some substance and you have
to keep them thinned properly to prevent them from caking.
They will have a tendency to dry up on the sly; one day you
have a bottle of nice opaque white ink, the next morning it's
a jar of white powder.

Whenever possible, drawings should be done on separate
sheets and then pasted in. But there are times when it
serves your purpose to draw right on the paste-up, for example to do an informal border around a page. You can
sketch the design in with a blue pencil and proceed carefully. Avoid drawing across pieces of the paste-up because
you may want to move them for some reason.

It is not always possible to have illustrations drawn to
exactly the size you need for the job--for example, about

half the drawings in this book were reduced to fit the particular requirements of the page. To have the printer make these various reductions would require many separate camera shots and extra stripping. However, it is possible to have photostats, or "stats," made by a commercial graphic arts cameraman. These stats are made with cheaper materials than used for printing work, so the quality of the stat is not as perfect as it might be if stripped into the job as a negative. But the savings are generally worth the insignificant reduction in quality.

At this point you are almost ready to take your paste-up to a printer. Burnish the entire job; hold a piece of tissue or newsprint (not newspaper) over the work to avoid marring it. Pick up excess rubber cement from around all edges with the rubber cement pickup, and white out any stray black marks. Spray with a fixative. Cover the work with a piece of paper folded over the top edge of the board and taped to the back. If you use a fancy colored paper and write the name of the job in your best calligraphic style, you will be a credit to any art director.

In the following chapters we will explore refinements and more exotic techniques, but using just what we've discussed till now you should be able to produce lively and inexpensive printed work.

6|Aspects of the Paste-up

There is no particular order in which to put the many details belonging in this chapter, since their only reason for being together at all is their relation to the basic paste-up discussed in Chapter 5. I will try to move from the more essential to the more esoteric, so you get what you need as quickly as possible.

Halftones

The most common form of illustration in offset printing is the reproduction of photographs. But halftones are the sirens in a job that might otherwise be smooth sailing. They take more care in planning and printing than line work, and you have to know something of the process to choose photographs that will reproduce well. As mentioned in Chapter 3, they have to be shot separately from the line artwork, and so are an additional expense. But you will need them, if only to avoid typing a thousand words in justified columns.

It is not difficult to plan for halftones in your layout. You have to remember that when a halftone is shot the camera does not drop out white or pale blue areas as it does with line shots. Everything will be seen as some shade of gray,

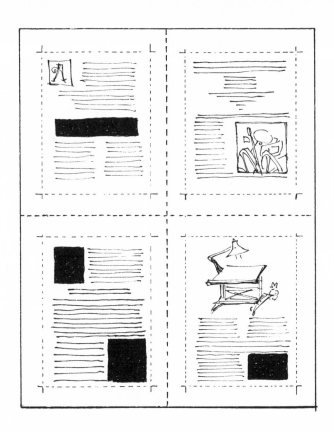

including the border of the picture and the copyboard of the camera. To define the desired limits of the picture paste a "window" of the proper size onto your layout. The material used is a red sticky-backed sheet called "Rubylith." It comes on a waxed paper backing and is transferred to the layout in much the same way as Art-type. The same material is also available mounted on acetate, for purposes I'll discuss later. The red sheet photographs as black, but you can see through it, which helps in positioning.

To make a window, first draw on the paste-up the shape and size you want the photograph to appear in blue pencil.

Cut a piece of Rubylith slightly larger all around than that shape, lay it over the drawing and burnish lightly. Then, using the line gauge and a sharp razor blade, carefully cut through the Rubylith along the pencil lines. The excess will pull right off the paste-up and the window can then be burnished firmly down. Rubylith is fragile and prone to tearing. Also a dull blade can tear little chunks off and make rough edges. As with type, the camera sees any mistakes--and you are striving for a crisp definition to the halftone, so extra care is necessary. When the entire paste-up is shot the window is just that: a clear rectangle (or square or whatever) in the negative. The halftone, shot separately, is taped down behind the window in its proper position. Windows can be any shape, since essentially what the window does is frame the halftone. Circles and complex shapes can be created in the same way as boxes. Just remember that the halftone has to fill the window completely, with enough room for taping. Black paper can be used for windows as well as Rubylith, but it is harder to fit into your paste-up, and the cut edges tend to be rough. It will certainly do in a pinch.

In preparing your paste-up to include halftones you must keep in mind that since the halftones will be shot separately, you will need some means of identification to see that the right picture goes in the right place. I generally use a letter code, marked on the back of the picture and in black behind the Rubylith on the layout. Whoever places the negatives can scratch the letters in a corner of the halftones and then use the paste-up as a guide. I also find it useful to put a short description of the picture in the window as well as the letter: something like, "A, two cows." Since none of this will be seen by the camera you can say anything you want.

The next problem in laying out halftones is the size and shape problem. Rarely will you find that the originals are the size or shape you need for the job. This means you will have to reduce or (less likely) enlarge the photograph, or crop it to the size desired. Using a proportional scale, it is an easy matter to plan the reduction or enlargement of the original to fit your layout. The proportional scale is a set of discs, graduated on their outer edges. To figure a reduction you line up the length of one side of the original with the desired length of the same side when reduced. A third scale then shows the percentage of reduction. A picture reduced from 10 inches to 8 inches would be reduced to 80% of its original size. That is the indication you put on the photograph when having it shot. If, on the other hand, the photograph does not have the proportions you desire, you must crop it to fit, and possibly reduce it as well. Two L shaped pieces of layout board can be used to frame the photograph and be moved around until the proportions and cropping are correct. I prefer to use "crop marks" at the edges of the photograph rather than cutting it, even if the print is expendable, because if you make an error you may have cut off a part you will need. Use a grease pencil (or China marker). It doesn't harm the photo, and can be wiped off if you make a mistake. You may want to cut a window of the right size in a sheet of paper to lay over the photograph as a quick guide to the crop when placing the halftone. A device called the Brandt Scaleograph figures cropping as well as reductions, but costs $14.00 and seems worth the money only if you are going to be doing an awful lot of work with halftones.

One of the most demanding skills in planning and designing print is choosing good photographs for reproduction. It takes experience, mostly, and a lot of looking at printed work. But here are a few pointers that should help you pick good halftones. Remember, from the description in Chapter 3, that a halftone creates the illusion of tonal range by actually printing only part of the picture. The more subtle the photograph the more technically difficult it is to reproduce as a halftone. So you can avoid a good deal of potential trouble by choosing, whenever possible, photographs that have simple, limited and clearly defined tonal values. You should avoid those pictures that are uniformly gray, and especially avoid those that concentrate on dark tones. On the other hand it is also wise to avoid pictures with an extremely wide tonal range--from absolute white to absolute black--as the halftone screen naturally tends to put some dot pattern in even the whitest or darkest area, and to drop out those dots to maintain the integrity of the photograph requires extra work on the part of the cameraman. Jim Wehlage of Sadhana Press suggests that your photographs all fall as much as possible within the same tonal range, as cameramen like to gang shots together whenever possible, which saves money, and they can achieve a uniform quality of negative throughout the work. Printed work will then have the same uniformity of tone which is pleasing in many cases, and the pressman will certainly have an easier time.

The reproduction of photographs can be a highly specialized craft that some people spend their lives perfecting. Those cameramen and pressmen who reproduce the work of Ansel Adams or the Sierra Club photographers, for example, have skills and training that none of us is expected to acquire within the scope of this book. Even if the few guidelines listed above work for you, the first thing you'll discover is that you seldom can pick and choose your photographs as these guidelines imply you can. It will happen that all you have to illustrate a leaflet with is a rectangle of dark gray mud, and you'll have to live with it. The best advice I can give on how to become an expert on halftones is to save a copy of everything you print along with the original art work and photo. This won't give you any absolute information, but it will show you tendencies, and discussion of the problems you are having with your cameraman or printer (or reflection on those problems if you're printing for yourself) will help you judge in advance what will happen to a given picture when it is printed. Then at least you will know when you're going to end up with mud and will be better able to deal with it.

Unfortunately a discussion of halftones doesn't end with the problems, but must go on to include some of the many variations on the halftone. A tricky problem printers run into, especially when printing political work, is the reproduction of previously printed photographs, such as those lifted from newspapers, magazines, and so on. To reprint these photos usually requires a process called *rescreening*. It is generally impossible to reprint the existing screen in the photo; even though it is in solid blacks and solid whites the presswork and paper have muddied the dot.

You must screen it anew as if it were a continuous tone photo, only placing the screen in such a way that it doesn't create a disturbing pattern of circular dark areas where the two sets of dots intersect. This pattern is called a *moire*. Usually it's minimized by looking at the subject through smoked glass placed on the back of the camera with the halftone screen over it. The screen is tilted around until the moire is at its least, the position marked, the smoked glass removed, and then with the screen in the marked position the photo is shot as an ordinary halftone. Wehlage claims that by shooting the subject slightly out of focus you can further minimize the moire, but you will lose some detail, and the halftone won't be exactly the same size as the original. Often reprints that should be rescreened are shot as if they were line copy and thus the resulting muddiness or ghosty dropped-out images you see in many leaflets. While the harsh truth of a photograph is graphically very powerful, it would be better to create a line rendering of the photo rather than print an illegible picture. Try sketching a newspaper photograph to see if you can capture the tone of it before you go through the trouble of rescreening.

Another kind of work involving tricky halftones is artwork that, while it is called black and white, really includes gray "washes" that have to be shot as halftones. This is especially true of illustrations done in brush and ink. Since you don't want a gray box which you get if you treat the whole illustration as a halftone, you have to make a *drop-out* halftone. This requires two camera shots, and often a good deal of hand work (expensive!). First a line shot is made of the artwork. The high-contrast quality of this negative drops out the shades of the paper and leaves only the darker tones of the illustration. It takes some skill to do this properly, and often unwanted spots will have to be carefully masked by hand. Then a halftone shot of the illustration is made and the two negatives are taped together. You can see poor examples of this process in the newspapers when there is a photo of a girl against a white ground and she has a silhouette like a paper doll. The effect of a good drop-out halftone is striking but the process is costly and difficult, and I suggest avoiding it.

Finally, I must mention that there are many special effects available to the person printing halftones, including second color possibilities (I will talk about full color reproduction later) and different screens from the ordinary--the mezzotint screen has been popular for the last few years. It reproduces dark and light tones in what appear to be random patterns, and creates more the effect of a painting than of a photograph. If you have gone that far in the reproduction of photographs you can better get the information from your printer or, if you are on your own, from a supplier such as Kodak.

Color

Nothing dresses up a printed piece like a second color, but caution is advised because adding color to your work adds considerably to your cost. Each color run adds the cost of a negative, plate, press run, and press wash up to the cost of running a single color only. The use of color is often the easy way out of a problem that should be solved by better designing. Before resorting to a second color you should explore the possibilities of large type, artwork, tone screens (mentioned later), novel placement of type on the page, or a single colored ink on a colored paper.

Planning type in a second color is a simple matter. Paste up the job as if it were to be in one color only. Tape a tissue over the work and mark the areas to be printed in color. The cameraman makes one negative, then masks it so that only the first color is exposed. When the plate is made of the first color he masks it off and exposes the second color. The tissue overlay acts as his guide, and the separate colors stay in perfect register since they were pasted up together. This method will work for any second color work as long as the separation is distinct and the colors do not overlap. Additional colors can be included in the same way.

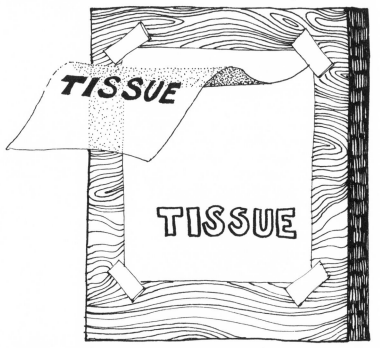

For very close work and for second colors in illustrations, another method is used in which the artist rather than the cameraman creates the separation. The basic black artwork is pasted on a board and two register marks, usually a cross or a cross in a circle, are placed at opposing points at the

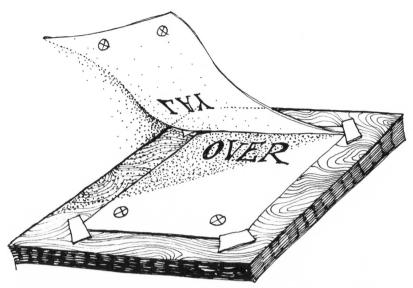

edge of or outside of the image area. A sheet of acetate is taped to the head of the board and register marks made on the acetate superimposed exactly on the basic marks. Prepared acetate is treated to accept ink, so you merely ink in the areas you want in a second color. You can also use Rubylith, the red masking sheets mounted on acetate, mentioned above. The Rubylith sheet is taped to the board and register marks are indicated. The outline of the image desired is cut in the Rubylith and the rest of the mask is peeled off the acetate, leaving it clear. There is a special swivel knife available for cutting Rubylith, and with practice you can cut very delicate shapes. I have never been able to make the thing work properly, and prefer a very sharp pointed X-acto knife. Look around art supply stores for possible tools. There are transfer type sheets that have register marks you can transfer to both the paste-up and the overlay just as you would type. There are also register marks on rolls like transparent tape. If a third color is desired a second overlay can be added in the same way as the first. The most complicated separations I have seen had a base color and seven overlays for a series of eight color greeting cards.

When color separations are photographed the cameraman first folds the overlay back and shoots the basic artwork, including the register marks. Then a piece of white paper is placed between the overlay and the base, and the second color shot, again including the register marks. The marks make it possible to put both negatives in exactly the same position in the masks. If the work is to be trimmed after printing the marks are usually left on the plates during both runs to insure proper register. If there is not room for a trim the pressman will run some sheets with the marks in the first color, then scrub them off the plate for the rest of the run. Those first sheets are then used to establish the position of the second color by lining up both sets of register marks. The marks on the second color plate are then scrubbed off.

Process Color

More people than you would imagine have the notion that if you draw a color the reproduction will be that color, transferred by some mysterious many-hued magical device. I once overheard this conversation between a printer and a young customer:

"I'd like to get this drawing printed."

"But this is a full-color illustration."

"Yep. Seventeen of 'em."

In order to reproduce watercolors, paintings, or photographs in color it is necessary to create the *illusion* of a wide spectrum of colors while using a limited number of colors. The colors used are similar to primary colors and when printed in juxtaposition with one another create the effect of mixed primaries. Thus an area printed in yellow and red will produce the effect of orange without actually printing orange ink. With the three primaries and black this effect can be extended clear across the tonal range. To print any full-color subject the job must be run through the press four times. The negatives are produced by a combination of filters to select out of the subject the four basic colors. Four negatives and plates are needed. The negatives are called *color separations* and are very expensive. In this area a set of color separations under 8 1/2 x 11 inches costs about $125.00. That doesn't include any plates or press work. If you need to get into four-color work you will learn it. I insert this note so that you won't be misled into thinking you can do full-color work as simply as the other methods we are discussing.

Bleeds

A bleed is a graphic effect in which one or more sides of a picture run off the edge of the page, or into the fold (gutter) of a book or magazine. In order to bleed an image the press sheet has to be printed oversize and then trimmed. You must plan for this sheet and subsequent trim when doing the paste-up. For example, if you are printing an 8 1/2 x 11 inch flyer and want to bleed a photo on two sides of the sheet, you must remember two important things; first, you must run a sheet larger than 8 1/2 x 11 inches, so you can't use pre-cut stock. If you buy 23 x 35 inch stock and cut it down you will get a sheet 8 3/4 x 11 1/2 inches which is enough margin for your bleed. Second, remember that all presses must have some *gripper margin*, that is the narrow area at the head of the sheet by which it is carried through the press. If the bleed is at the top of the page you must design your work so that the top 1/4 to 3/8 inch can be cut off. This is true as well for an image that comes very close to the top edge but does not bleed. In no case can you print within that gripper margin, and to get close to the top edge of a sheet you must print it oversize. Your printer will tell you how much gripper to allow if you are planning a job of this sort. In pamphlet work you must be careful when bleeding a photograph across the fold, especially if the two pages do not print on the same sheet, as careful stripping and press-work is required to see that the two sides match.

Double Burns

Interesting effects can be created by the use of type directly over a photograph, for example on a pamphlet cover. Since the type and photo are shot separately you have to expose the type image onto the plate after the halftone image is made.

This makes a solid area where there is type, leaving the halftone around it. In designing this combination you can either mount the type on a clear acetate overlay and indicate a double burn or deliver the type on a separate sheet and use a tissue over the photo to indicate its position.

Reverses

An opposite effect is sometimes desired, in which the type is in white, or reverse, in a halftone or in a solid block of color. Generally this is done by making a separate reverse negative after the original negative is shot. This reverse negative appears as black type on clear film, and the film must be large enough to cover the entire area the type is reversed into, so that the edges of the film won't show on the plate. This extra work can be costly, especially if a very large area of clear film is necessary. By using transfer type on acetate the same effect as a reverse negative is gained which can be used directly in the platemaking process, avoiding two camera processes. It is possible to use white transfer type on Rubylith, black paper, or even directly on a photograph, but there is still a camera shot. I have never been too pleased with the results of white transfer lettering.

Mechanical Screens

In order to create the effect of shades in an illustration, or to make type gray, mechanical screens are used that produce the same result as a halftone screen but permit a set tonal value rather than a series of graduated tones depending on the color range of the subject. To avoid confusing these mechanical screens with a halftone screen I'll use the term *screen tint*. Tints are most commonly prepared at the stripping and platemaking stage, especially when type is to be screened. Screen tints are in the form of negatives graduated in percentage of solid color, from 90% of solid down to 10%. A 50% screen would be exactly half black and half white and would screen the subject to a medium gray color. The screen is taped behind the material you want screened the same way a halftone is taped to a window. You must beware of two things. First, be sure that the screen covers only the area you want it to. It's frustrating to notice that the screen tint cuts across part of the text after the plate is made and on the press. Second, check that the screen tint is not too light or too dark for the job. Examine tints and notice how light a 10% screen is and how dark a 90% screen is. In many cases a 90% screen would be indistinguishable from solid black, and a 10% screen almost invisible. To indicate a screen tint on the paste-up you would use a tissue overlay, marking the areas to be screened and giving the percentage tint to be used.

Screen tints are available as transfer sheets for use directly on the paste-up. As mechanicals their generic name is BenDay, after (who else) Ben Day, a New York printer working around the turn of the century who invented a machine to create shaded effects in engravings. BenDays are used to a great extent in the preparation of commercial artwork. Use it as you do Rubylith in an overlay, placing the screen over the illustration, cutting around the area you want shaded, then burnishing. (See illustration, p. 113.) Unless you are particularly clever with a blade, you can't use BenDays to shade type, since it's hard to cut around the outlines of finer letters, and you must revert to film screens.

Now here is the fun part of BenDay tints. The variety of shading effects you can get with transfer sheets defies imagination. I just checked the catalog from a local art supply store and found among many others: graduated screens that range from 10% to 90%, line screens, screens for use by architects (brick patterns), map-makers (treetops), special screens (pinwheels, tweed, wavy lines). You shouldn't stock up on those exotic screens but they certainly can suggest possibilities.

Calligraphy

At the very beginning of this book I rhapsodized on the revival of calligraphy and its sound use as a contemporary graphic medium. It's not an especially easy craft to learn. I have practiced it for some time and am still awfully clumsy. I don't propose to teach it, but I have listed some excellent sources in the bibliography. What I want to emphasize here is that pens and inks are highly versatile tools to have around your studio, and, whether you want to involve yourself with the craft of handwriting or not, you should acquaint yourself with the uses of the many pens available. Even better, keep them around and play with them. (I should interject that a selection of brushes is also very handy to use with white or black ink for touching up art, simple illustration work, etc.) Here are a few of the most common pens:

OSMIROID: The most popular of the calligraphic pens, and while professionals find it inadequate and cranky, it is inexpensive and easy to find. Many nibs are available. Keep the pen clean, don't leave it filled with India inks, and it should stay useful. For under $5.00 you can get a pen and several nibs. Then get the *Puffin Book of Lettering* (see bibliography) and start playing around.

RAPIDOGRAPH: Most of us are familiar with the Rapidograph pen. Used extensively by illustrators, it creates a line of constant width, and the different points available allow the user to vary the line from extremely thin to quite fat. If the Osmiroid is cranky, the Rapidograph is mulish. That fellow you see with a big pad of paper on his knee who

appears to be shaking with a palsy of the hand is trying to make his Rapidograph work. Chuck Miller has used a Rapidograph almost entirely in illustrating this book, and tells of the time he drove one half way through a layout table, piqued at the pen's recalcitrance. A complete Rapidograph outfit, with all eight points, three holders, ink bottles, etc., all in a Humidifier Revolving Selector, costs $27.00. The pen alone costs about $5.00. Since these pens are intended to be used with India ink, the bulk of their attendant problems involves the ink drying out and clogging the pen, hence the Humidifier Revolving Selector. Keeping the pen clean is of supreme importance, and if you are using it only as an occasional tool I would suggest cleaning it after each use. With any of these pens you learn what you can get away with after a little experience.

STEEL PENS: Those scratchy blotty things with which many of us learned penmanship in school. They may be hateful but they're cheap and great for an informal kind of scratchy blotty drawing or lettering.

SPEEDBALL PENS: The mainstay of lettering pens. With a wide range of nib styles including steel brushes up to 3/4 inch wide, it's a good idea to have a whole jar full of nibs around. Ordinary nibs cost a quarter, and the big steel brushes a dollar. The nibs are not very finely made; in smaller italic sizes not nearly as well as Osmiroid nibs, but the square, round, and oval nibs are pretty much exclusive to Speedball, and while they may not seem to have any obvious utility, they fall into our classification of handy possibilities.

RULING PENS: (Also known as the Precision Roach Clip.) These come in a variety of styles, but they all are basically two adjustable crablike pincers. Ink is held between the two sides and the width of line is determined by the distance be-

tween the two jaws. They are tricky to use, as the ink has a tendency to flow out all at once, and all you can draw with them is a straight line. But they are important to know about because they are the best kind of pen to use with a straightedge. Other pens tend to smear along the edge of the ruler, making it hard to draw a clean straight line. Also the width of the line is instantly variable. Get one and play with it. It only costs $1.50.

There are a lot of other pens available, different brands and pens that do different things. You should scout around to see what there might be that you can use.

The Clip File

Most of us have a tendency to accumulate pictures, drawings, or photos that we find funny, compelling, or sentimental. The graphic designer can turn this tendency into a cornucopia of material for his leaflets and pamphlets by organizing his little quirk. Back at the beginning we found that anything you can photograph you can print, so you can snip, steal, borrow, trace, sketch, and generally use all the efforts that have gone before you as grist for the work you are producing. *Kayak Magazine,* which should be studied for its fantastic homemade graphics, has made tremendous use of nineteenth century engravings from all kinds of sources: astrology, anatomy, botany texts, old novels, and encyclopedias have all been used to lend mind-boggling illustrations to contemporary surrealist poetry.

7 Paper & Ink

The greatest single resource the impecunious printer has to work with is paper. Paper is as basic to a printed piece as the original layout, and should be as carefully planned as any other aspect of the job. Time spent learning about paper, its history, manufacture, varieties, etc., will certainly not be wasted, since, over the long run, paper may be your largest single expense. Learning the most economical use of paper for your purposes and the many sources for paper in your area can help you avoid much unnecessary expense.

In defining paper Dard Hunter, the great authority on papermaking, said: "To be classed as true paper, the thin sheets must be made from vegetable fibre that has been macerated until each individual filament is a separate unit: the fibres lifted from the water in the form of a thin stratum, leaving a sheet of matted fibre upon the screen's surface. This layer of intertwined fibre is paper." (From *Papermaking, the History of an Ancient Craft.*)

The vegetable fibers can be of any cellulose, but generally cotton, linen, bamboo, esparto grass, or wood are used; with wood being by far the most common in the United States. And there simplistic description ends and a good share of magic enters. For the making of paper is a process virtually unchanged since its beginning in China a hundred years after the birth of Christ. The Fourdrinier paper-making machines in use today don't do anything basically different from the vatman in a Medieval mill lifting his screen, or mold, up through the fibers suspended in water, and pressing the water out of the sheets on a screw press.

No matter how the paper is formed, something changes in the process that makes a sheet of paper something other than a mat of cellulose fibers, just as the ink and type of a printing press, the folds and covers of the binding, make the sheet of paper something other than paper--all part of the process that leads to the analogy of bookmaking as architecture. And the part-time amateur printer with a Multilith is no less involved in the magic that begins with the subtle changing of fibers on a wire screen than is the finest book printer or artist of an engraving or lithograph. For what he creates must be just as much unified with the paper, the ink, the design, and the purpose to produce a whole that neglects none of its parts.

Public libraries generally have enough material to get an understanding of the making of paper, and any book by Dard Hunter (see bibliography) is not only filled with useful information, but also gives some hint as to where the magic comes from. Books printed before 1800 (when the papermaking machine became common) will give you a look at handmade papers, and some art supply stores have samples of modern handmade art papers. Looking at and handling handmade paper will give you knowledge of and sensitivity to the papers you will use every day, just as studying fine types and typography will help you create handsome things with a typewriter.

Buying Paper

The varieties of color, texture, and weight in contemporary papers is tremendous, due primarily to the fact that the paper mills are in stiff competition to grab the attention of advertising designers, and so are always coming up with new colors and textures to catch the eye. Even in the cheaper papers, the vellum bristols, the bonds, the mimeo papers, the range of colors is growing all the time. The best way to utilize this variety is to begin acquiring paper companies' sample swatches, and collecting printed samples that use papers you find appealing. These samples can then be shown to a paper salesman who can tell you the kind of paper and its source. Another way to explore the possibilities of paper is through "close-out" paper houses. These firms buy up paper from printers going out of business, damaged shipments, fire sales, etc., and resell it at very low prices. Usually you can rummage around the warehouse and look for the odd bits and pieces that are just right for the job, or an unexpected paper that suggests new possibilities.

On the west coast there is a chain of paper companies, called Arvey Paper Co., that sells on a cash and carry basis, and operates much like a supermarket--you can browse around to find what you want. There is probably a firm like this in your area, and you will find that it is less expensive than a regular wholesaler for small quantities. I have found papers at Arvey to be of lower quality than those from a wholesaler, but for certain jobs they are exactly right. Arvey has a paper called Tru-Ray that comes in an astounding range of colors. Other sources will suggest themselves as you explore the possibilities. For example, large printers might be talked out of end cuts from big jobs.

For general paper buying (for paper used all the time, such as bonds and book papers), I have found it works out best to find a good general wholesaler and use him for everything. This way you will find it easier to establish credit, get samples, and an up-to-date price book, and regular deliveries. (The price book is an essential tool and you can learn a lot about paper just from reading it.)

The one restriction of this method is that no wholesaler handles papers from all manufacturers and so may not have a particular paper you are looking for. On the other hand, papers generally don't vary so much that you can't find a substitute that will serve, and any wholesaler will fill a one-time cash order. Remember, when looking for a wholesaler to work with, that the larger the company the more likely you are to end up dealing with a computer, and the less likely are the people you do talk to to know much about paper. Salesmen have a tendency to be able to sell anything, and their presence in a paper company does not insure their expertise. So look around for a company that has a selection of papers you like, and people on the staff you can work with. If you are printing or planning print over a long period, a good relationship with a paper company will save you a lot of time and many hassles.

The specific knowledge you need concerning the paper you use is in two areas: the different classifications of paper; and the different sizes that will fit your press.

Varieties of Paper

While there are scores of specialty papers available, which you may at some point find a use for, the kinds of paper you will use for almost all your work are: bond paper, book or text paper, and cover paper.

BOND PAPER: Bonds are traditionally considered writing papers. They are made to be printed as letterheads and are sold in the standard 8 1/2 x 11 inch and 8 1/2 x 14 inch letter sizes as well as in full sheets. The quality varies from a very cheap sulphite grade up to fine sheets made of 100% cotton fiber. Because they are pre-cut and come in such a price range, they are the papers used in small job shops for flyers, handbills, etc. Until recently the colors available were always pastels (apparently because of the notion that letters were more easily read on light colors), but in the

last few years more and more colors have been added, and
there are now bonds available in brilliant shades such as
chartreuse and hot pink. ("Earth" colors were the vogue a
few years back, and there are still a lot of those around.)
The finish on bonds ranges from smooth and rather plain in
the cheaper grades, through ripples and cockles to the fine
laid lines of a good letterhead paper. The weights are 16 lb.,
20 lb., and, less frequently, 24 lb., with 20 lb. being the
all around useful weight. A 16 lb. paper is of course cheaper, but it's too translucent to print well on both sides, and
as it is not as stable as 20 lb. paper, it has been known to
cause trouble in feeding through the press. (The weights of
paper listed in this chapter are "basis weights," the actual
weight of 500 sheets of the paper in its full size. They indicate relative thicknesses.) Because of their price, you will
find that bonds will always be your mainstay papers, and
one of your roughest challenges as the designer of low-cost
printing is to make a job on dollar-a-ream white sulphite
look exciting.

BOOK AND TEXT PAPERS: The middle grade book paper
is of a little higher quality than a good sulphite bond and
tends to be a bit bulkier and softer. This classification includes the workhorse papers you find in offset brochures,
annual reports, and some magazines. It also covers the
vast array of colors and finishes found in the text papers.
Here is where the paper mills have gone all out to capture
the business of the designers, and most mills have a prime
grade text paper in several weights including covers, and
with an extensive range of colors. Many can be had with
rough deckle edges for fancy jobs. It must be remembered
that, while the colors and finishes of the text papers are
more immediately appealing than bonds and standard book
papers, they are also a good deal more expensive, and you
should avoid becoming enamored of a pretty text paper when
the job would be just as good and cheaper on a bond or book
paper with a little extra imagination.

The weights of standard book paper vary from 50 lb. to
100 lb., with 60 lb. being generally comparable to 20 lb.
bond. Text papers are generally 70 lb. or 80 lb.

To indicate how much variation there is in the amount you
can spend on paper for even the simplest job: a ream (500
sheets) of good 20 lb. sulphite bond, 8 1/2 x 11 inches costs
$2.78. A comparable 60 lb. book costs $3.20 for the same
size and amount. An inexpensive text paper, 70 lb. weight
but for the same size and amount, costs $4.05, and could
cost as much as $5.90, or better than twice the price of
a ream of good bond. These prices are all for white paper.
Colors are always a little higher, but the comparisions are
still the same.

An additional consideration in ordering book and text papers is that they very seldom are sold in pre-cut sizes, and
your paper company will charge you for cutting the full size
sheets (see below).

COVER PAPERS: A cover paper could be considered anything from 100 lb. book paper on up to multi-ply boards,
but generally is about the same weight as you find on most
paperbacks. Textures and colors of cover stocks vary as
much as do bonds and book papers, and most text papers
have a matching or compatible series of covers to go with
them. A light weight cover is 65 lb., and most work is done
on 80 lb. or 100 lb. Prices vary as much as they do for the
lighter weights, and you have to consider cutting in most
cases.

Since cover stock is generally more expensive than text
weights when planning a printed piece it is wise to consider
whether you actually need the heavier weight. For example
I recently printed a small (24 page) poetry pamphlet using
70 lb. book stock for the cover as well as for the inside. I
was able to avoid a separate run on the press as the cover
was just part of the large press sheet. This also saved on
bindery costs, and so far none of the copies I have seen suf-
fered any damage from being unprotected.

RECYCLED PAPER: I find recycled paper no harder to use
than ordinary paper. It is a bit more expensive than bonds,
but cheaper than middle-grade book paper. I even used it to
type the manuscript of this book. Watch out however for recycled paper that isn't rigidly color-controlled (e. g., Bergstrom Recycle 100). We have a carton in the shop that al-
ternates gray-white, blue-white, and old rose throughout
the carton. If you are doing good book or pamphlet work it
won't do, although it's fine for leaflets and broadsides. There
is a sheet from Bergstrom called Conserv-opaque that is
a bright white, and Mead makes a good recycled book paper
of a consistent off-white color.

Paper Sizes

I mentioned that most bonds come pre-cut to 8 1/2 x 11 inches or 8 1/2 x 14 inches, and that book, text, and cover
papers have to be cut from full-size "mill sheets." While
there are many different standard mill sizes, especially if
you work at all with European or Oriental papers, there are
really only four basic sizes used in offset printing. The following chart shows the standard sizes of paper, the size
press sheet for a small offset press, and in three cases the
size book or pamphlet the paper will make after trimming.

Paper	Press Sheet	Trimmed Book
8 1/2 x 11	pre-cut	
8 1/2 x 14	pre-cut	
17 1/2 x 22 1/2	8 1/2 x 11 press sheet	5 1/2 x 8 1/2 book
23 x 29	11 x 14 1/2 press sheet*	
23 x 35	double 17 1/2 x 22 1/2	
25 x 38	9 1/2 x 12 1/2 press sheet	6 x 9 book
26 x 40	10 x 13 press sheet	6 1/2 x 10 book
	*maximum for a small duplicator	

As you can see by the chart, many of the sizes you will find in a paper price book are multiples of smaller sizes. You will notice in the price book that one of the dimensions is underlined. This indicates grain direction in the paper, a characteristic in all machine-made papers caused by the fibers being moved along in one direction by the papermaking machine. This grain affects folding properties, and if you're planning a book or pamphlet, you should see that the fold is along the grain, to assure ease of opening and help the book lie flat when opened. You will notice that pre-cut stock usually has the grain running the long way, which is wrong if you intend to make a pamphlet by folding the short way (say 5 1/2 x 8 1/2 inches out of 8 1/2 x 11 inches). But you will notice that 23 x 35 inch stock usually has the grain running the long way as well, and if you cut 8 1/2 x 11 inch stock out of it for your pamphlet the grain will run the right direction. You can determine the grain direction easily by folding the sheet. It will fold smoothly along the grain, but against the grain folding is more difficult.

In planning cutting, especially for jobs that aren't the ordinary sizes, the greatest problem is waste. It's not hard to waste as much as 10% of your paper in making special cuts, and you can end up with narrow strips you either have no use for or which are too small to run on the press. Often this waste is impossible to avoid, but in order to counter the mindless overproduction of most printed matter much energy should go into keeping an empty waste bin. Waste strips can be used over and over; the backs can be used for your kid's drawings or letters to your folks. And careful planning can keep you from having to figure out all those creative uses for scrap.

Here is an example: Most small offset presses will handle a sheet 10 x 15 inches and it is often demanded that you push the press to that limit, to do posters and such that need to be as large as possible. But looking at the paper price book you will notice that there is no parent sheet that will yield a 10 x 15 inch sheet without waste. The best you can do is

23 x 35 inches which will yield a lot of 3 inch strips, which are practically useless, and a 5 inch strip. If you cut a 10 x 14 1/2 inch sheet out of a 23 x 29 inch sheet you will still get the 3 inch strip. So try to plan the job for 10 x 13 inches (out of 26 x 40 inches), 8 1/2 x 14 inches, or go up to 11 x 17 inches (out of 23 x 35 inches) and have the press work done for you. (Once again, you are dealing with a limitation as a creative force. When I complained to Frank Westlake, the great and zany San Francisco printer, that I needed a press larger than I had, he said, "Forget it. You could have a 50 inch press and somebody would come along with a 51 inch job.")

When ordering paper keep a close watch on the quantities you are ordering and the relative price. Paper companies give a tremendous price break for whole cartons, and you can save a lot of money by planning ahead enough to take advantage of a lower price. I just checked my price book and found that seven reams of Nekoosa bond would cost me $21.42, while ten reams would cost only $21.10! Paper salesmen probably will never call your attention to these price breaks, so take the time to check before placing an order. Also notice in your price book that you can use certain assortments to get the quantity discount, enabling you to stock up for contingencies. And always remind yourself that you pay a penalty for small orders. A good way to buy small quantities is to use the close-out houses, or paper "supermarkets," I mentioned above. The price is usually the same regardless of quantity, so you are not penalized. But you tend to pay more than necessary for large quantities for the same reason. Printing always seems to be under insurmountable time pressures, and it is hard to take the time to explore alternatives and possibilities when the deadline is standing at the door. But careful planning pays, as I have said and will doubtless say again, and it doesn't take too many "free" reams of paper on quantity orders to add up to enough for a whole job.

The final problem to consider in the realm of paper is

the advisability of a cutter. I will have more to say about this under the "Starting a Shop" chapter, but a discussion of the problem is appropriate here. In your price book you will notice that it costs $5.00 to $15.00 to have one thousand parent sheets cut down to fit a small press. This is a case where you are paying for labor you could do yourself, and it would be wise to relate the expense of this kind of cutting to the cost of a paper cutter. Another concern is the utilization of end cuts and waste. Only by having a cutter handy can you make effective use of long strips, old letterheads, etc.

Ink

Since ink is the other "raw material" used in the creation of a printed piece, it is appropriate to talk about it in this chapter. If you look at books on printing, bookmaking, etc., about all you can find out about ink is that Gutenberg used boiled linseed oil with resin, soap, and lampblack tossed in. It turns out, as you dig into technical journals and talk to suppliers, that there is very little else to say about the composition of ink. It certainly isn't the magic thing that paper is. Despite greatly advanced chemistry and knowledge of pigments, driers, and other additives, ink is still the varnish-based stuff it was five hundred years ago. One interesting development is latex or rubber-based inks. Most offset printers love them, mainly because they don't set up on the press but dry quickly on the paper. I have also been using them for letterpress printing and, except for a lack of brilliance in the black, have found little to complain about.

The way to learn about inks is to print with them. The chemistry of the ink and water systems in offset printing is fairly complicated, and a problem on the press may be as much in the water fountain solution as the ink. A brand of ink enthused over by one printer will be found intractable by another. Recently inks have been developed specifically for use with photo-direct plates such as Itek, and for other special needs of offset printers. You should discuss your particular situation with your supplier.

Our real concern here is the use of ink with paper to create strength and effectiveness in your printed work. If the use of a colored paper can perk up a job that was sinking into drabness, printing the text in the right colored ink on colored paper can wing the job into excitement. There are a couple of guides you can use in picking colors. The "Coloron" set, available from art supply houses for about $10.00, is a small portfolio of twelve transparent plastic sheets with screened colors and type. It will give you some idea of how colors will work together and how type will work on color, but it is obviously restricted in use. Have a look at one and see if it's worth $10.00 to you. The second chart I consider an essential if you are working with commercial printers, and damn handy if you're printing on your own. It is the PMS color mixing system, a chart showing over 500 different colors with formulas for mixing each of them from ten basic colors. The use of this system has grown to the extent that you can specify a PMS color number to almost any printer and get the color you want. And the chart is a great idea resource, because you can fan it out to show a whole range of colors all together to see tones you might not have considered. I have seen them priced from $3.00 to $5.00.

As I've said before, you must allow experience to be your guide in learning what you can get away with in the use of color. And some people have a knack for color while others don't. Working at our shop is an artist who sees nuances of color that pass right by my ham-fisted eye. Whenever possible I defer to his judgment, or the judgment of anyone who has a talent for those things. This doesn't mean you can't go it on your own if you lack this sensibility; you just may not get the stunning, subtle effects of a master.

8 | Binding

I use "binding" as a general term for anything you do to a job after the actual printing, which includes collating, folding, and any of the ways you hold paper together: stapling, ring binding, sewing, and actual bookbinding. These operations tend to be overlooked in the planning and preparation of printed work, because they can be tedious and not nearly as exciting as designing or laying out the job. Hence many of the creative possibilities available in binding are overlooked.

Good commercial bindery equipment is very expensive and takes training to operate properly. Traditional hand-bookbinding, making use of fine papers and leathers, also requires skills, training, and some equipment. It is a craft demanding much time and study from its practitioners. The simple binding of small pamphlets and small case-bound books, however, is an area in which you don't have to have much money or specialized skills as long as you've got plenty of time. In my work I have chosen to send all operations that are too difficult or time-consuming to do by hand to professional binderies. In this chapter I will stress hand work, and recommend that you consider using professionals rather than investing in folding machines and wire stitchers.

Folding

Folding is the most common requirement. There are folding machines intended for office use that handle 8 1/2 x 11
inch sheets only, for as little as $100.00 to $125.00, and
a quality machine such as Challenge or Pitney-Bowes for
the same size runs something over $300.00. I have never
liked these office folding machines; of course the first thing
you'll need to fold will be 9 x 12 inches and already they
are useless. I used to use a Pitney-Bowes folder that could
fold a sheet up to 11 x 17 inches, and for smaller sheets it
worked pretty well. But they cost $875.00, a pretty hefty
investment. None of these smaller machines will fold anything more complicated than one or two parallel folds. You
can't, for example, fold a sheet one way and then across,
as you might if you were making an announcement or small
pamphlet. And of all the machines we've talked about, a
small folding machine is the most frustrating to operate.
It's better to spend your time drinking beer than weeping
and cursing over wrinkled sheets, crooked folds, inaccurate adjustments. I really believe it is worse to waste paper
than time, and those little folding machines can really waste
paper. Get a few friends together around a big table and a
couple of thousand leaflets can be folded by hand in no time.

To fold sheets by hand what you need is a folding bone.
These are bars of ivory, bone, or plastic about six inches
long, usually slightly curved, with all edges rounded. They
give a smooth surface and enough extra leverage to allow
a very tight clean crease when folding. The best bone fold-
ers only cost a dollar; plastic costs about forty cents. You
can use a big soup spoon and get the same result, or a ny-
lon comb or burnisher. But a real bone folder is a comfortable tool that one learns to love, like a good pen or a pocket
knife, and that kind of relationship is worth a dollar.

I will now tell you how to fold a sheet of paper, only because many people do it improperly, which results in bad
work. First, give yourself plenty of room on a clean hard

surface. Stack the sheets to be folded in such a way that you can take one off and fold the corner you're holding over onto the opposite corner. This saves turning and flopping the sheet each time to get it into the correct position. You should use the top of the job as your guide for folding. The two outer edges should line up with the top edge lining up all the way across. If the sheet has been cut crookedly, make sure the top edges line up even if it means the outer edges don't. Hold the sheet down firmly at the point where the two outside corners meet and with the other hand run the bone back toward the fold to avoid wrinkling, and then along the fold to complete it. If you do not hold the sheet down firmly the fold may go crooked, and you can never really unfold a sheet of paper. You can refold it properly, but the mark of the wrong fold will remain. To aid you in folding you can lubricate the folding bone by rubbing it occasionally alongside your nose; the oils on your skin make the folder slide more easily.

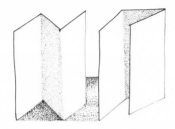

One of the most common leaflet forms is the standard letter fold: a sheet of 8 1/2 x 11 inch paper folded in thirds to make a leaflet 3 5/8 x 8 1/2 inches. To fold this sheet by hand you have to know where to make the first fold. When pasting up the job put a black dot somewhere along the line that will become the outer edge of the first fold. The dot will hardly be noticeable, and when the job is folded the workers just line up the top of the job, see that the outer edge meets the dot, then fold the other panel over to meet the crease of the first fold. The illustration shows two ways to make a three-panel fold: the standard letter fold and an accordion fold.

Another useful fold is called the "French fold." All it is, really, is a sheet folded in half, and then in half again the other way. What it lets you do, however, is make an announcement or small four-page folder by printing on only one side of the sheet of paper; the unprinted side is folded inside the announcement and isn't seen.

Other folds are used for binding pamphlets and books when they are printed on large presses. If you find yourself planning something this large you should check with your bindery before you do any layouts to get a pattern for the folds and the position of the pages on the press. If you are doing work of that size on your own equipment you don't need me anymore.

Collating

Gathering sheets together, or collating, is the next bit of manual work you'll have to get done after the fun of getting it printed is over. There are some amazing machines invented to help office slaves gather sheets of stock reports or whatever office slaves gather, but none of them actually does the work for you, they just help a little bit; you push a button or depress a lever and rollers push each sheet out of its little slot, and you scoop them all up. At the price they are just gadgets, like wax paper dispensers and electric can openers. The best device I have seen is an expanding rack like a miniature clothes dryer. The sheets are stacked at a slight angle and the operator moves his hand along flicking each sheet out of the rack. I've seen both wooden and metal racks like these and you should be able to get one by asking your supplier. There is one made by Evans for about $15.00. Lately any collating I have done I've used a book case of bricks and boards, stacking the sheets in their proper order. A big table can be used in the same way, and you just walk around the table.

Attaching

Next comes the problem of attaching miscellaneous gathered sheets together. The simplest form of binding is the staple, the venerable staple, attaching the sheets either at the upper left-hand corner or along the left side. In the days of the mimeograph magazines a cover would be stapled over the printed sheets and perhaps a strip of tape over the spine covered the staples. We all own staplers so there is your tool for binding of that sort. If you want to tape the spine use a colored mending tape available at stationers'.

The other stapling method requires some equipment. That is the method of stapling through a series of folded sheets to make a pamphlet. To staple pamphlets you need a "saddle stapler," one that has a V-shaped board to keep the folded sheets in position while stapling. Hand-operated staplers of this type cost from $14.00 to $45.00 depending on how heavy a load they are intended to handle. A standing foot-operated model, which leaves both hands free to manipulate the pamphlets (making the work go much faster), sells new for $125.00. They are readily available for half that used. Many of the larger staplers have convertible boards that allow you to handle either flat or folded sheets. Fancier yet is the electrically powered wire stitcher, but I can't figure out why anybody would want one at close to $600.00 new. Their advertising claims they are very fast.

In Chapter 9 I discuss the preparation of pamphlets. Here let me talk a bit about putting them together. Your pattern for collating will be determined by the design established when it is printed and you will be following a dummy provided by the printer. If the pamphlet is small all the sheets can be gathered and folded together at the same time. Proceed as with a single sheet, lining up all the tops of the sheets. You have to crease the fold very tightly and you will notice that the outer edges tend to bevel slightly. There is no way to avoid this but holding the sheets down tightly while folding will help minimize it. To really fold a pamphlet properly you should fold each sheet separately, and then insert them into each other in their proper order. This has to be

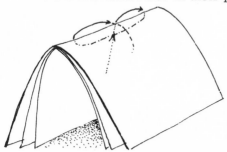

done if the pamphlet has more than six to eight sheets. In any case, the cover of a pamphlet, if of heavier stock, should be folded separately and the rest inserted. For all the small pamphlets we do at our press, we bind by hand sewing them, a process slower than stapling, but one that produces an elegant appearance more in the traditions of true bookbinding than staples. As the drawing shows, it is an easy technique to learn. The threaded needle is punched through the center of the folded book, starting from the inside fold, then the

needle comes back through the fold at one end. (You will
find it easier to punch a hole with the needle from the inside first, then go back and come through the outside.) The
thread is then stretched all the way along the fold and out a
hole at a similar point at the opposite end of the book. The
thread then comes back through the hole at the center, the
two ends are tied across the long thread down the center so
that the knot can't pull through and snipped off to leave a-
bout a half-inch end. A sewn book like this is actually more
durable than a stapled one, and no sheets can pull loose as
they sometimes do when stapled. The thread is unobtrusive
and doesn't bulge the spine as some staples do.

We found that punching the books ahead of time saves a
good deal of time in sewing. Use two boards nailed together
to form horizontal and vertical sides. The fold of the book
is placed in the V of the boards and the three holes punched
through the book toward the point of the V. For a punch use
a sharp awl or a large needle stuck in a wine cork. While
you are punching and sewing you may drink the wine. Don't
make the holes too large; you just want to help get the needle
through, so you don't have to punch too deeply. If you want the
holes to be consistently in the same place on all the pamphlets (a nice professional touch) use a cardboard template
with three points marked that you lay into the fold, lined up
with the top of the pamphlet. The thread should be button
and carpet thread, available wherever sewing supplies are
sold, for about 20 cents. There is a variety of colors available. Bindery supply houses sell various weights of linen
thread, which is used in commercial binding. This thread
is very strong and thin, and has a neutral color that makes
it less noticeable. A half-pound spool costs $3.75, which
is ultimately cheaper than button and carpet thread, and it's
good to have a big supply around if you are doing much pamphlet work. We use about a spool a year.

There are several ways to dress up a pamphlet. You can
make the cover larger than the text, which gives a colored
border around the pages when the book is open. Or you can

bind in a blank sheet of contrasting colored paper between the text and the cover to add interest. A way to hide the staples in a pamphlet is to staple the text together with a heavier sheet of blank colored paper. The cover is printed on a sheet long enough to leave flaps that can be folded around the blank outer sheet, much like the flaps of a dust jacket on a hard-bound book. The cover can be glued at the back to keep it from slipping off. For this style of binding the cover should be on lighter weight paper than the blank sheet.

Commercial binderies offer a wide range of more sophisticated bindery methods which should be explored as possible resources. Automatic pamphlet stitchers gather the folded sheets, staple, and trim them at amazing speed. Perfect binding machines for bookmaking trim the folds off the spine of a book and glue the individual sheets into the cover. This book is an example of that kind of binding, as are most paperbacks. There are machines for spiral binding and plastic ring binding, and the costs of these should be compared with other methods when considering a large project. Finally there are those firms which do traditional bookmaking of both hard-bound volumes and paperbacks, and they offer possibilities for gold and other metallic stamping, making portfolio covers using either cloth or paper, as well as fine quality binding.

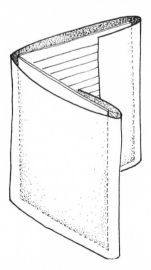

9|Planning Print

I want to set out a program for getting a printing job out of the author's head and into the streets. That involves rules and procedures and when I think of all the sets of rules and procedures that I've created for myself I'm reminded of the last job that got delayed for a week because I forgot to ask a client if he wanted it collated. Or the typographical error on the back cover of a recent book that was overlooked by the typesetter, the proofreader, the pressman, the publisher, *and* the author. But procedures do work to minimize these maddening situations, and maybe if I get them right this time I can stick to them.

And I want to reiterate my argument against the common separation of the "designer" from the "planner." The two are synonymous in meaning, inseparable in function, and a talent for clever layouts gives the designer no excuse to ignore the workings of the craft. The converse of this complaint could be levied against working printers who think that because they are not "artists" they are somehow excused from the creative aspects of their work. In fact, graphic designers could be said to have sprung up solely because printers weren't doing the whole job. I recently had a printer tell me that he considered himself a typographer, not a

99

designer, which is no better than considering one's self a
designer and not a typographer. One produces frilly non-
sense; the other yields hackneyed, dreary pages.

Before touching type to paper there are a series of steps
that will smooth the way once typesetting and paste-up have
gotten under way, and that will minimize resetting, repast-
ing, and hopefully errors.

1. Get the *complete* text of the job before doing anything.
Only by knowing what you have can you figure out what you
want. And it's better to wait till the manuscript is complete
than to waste time planning something that may have to be
changed completely.

2. Determine, by your own reading of the text, and by
discussion with its perpetrator, what form the work might
best take. (How, for example, does the author envision the
printed piece? Often the answers are very revealing.) If
you are in the position of having some part in the writing of
the piece you are printing, you have the enviable opportu-
nity to develop your ideas for the text and its printed form
simultaneously--and you can encourage changes in the text
that will make it better fit into the ideal format. A good example of this is that common situation where the text ends
up a line or so too long for its given space, no matter how
careful the planning. If, as is the case with many authors,
the text is sterling and inviolable, the poor designer can
only squeeze and pinch or reset some type. But if you have
some control over the text it's a simple matter to rewrite
a line or two to gain the space you need.

3. Establish a budget. This is not a futile exercise, even
if you are perpetually penniless. A discussion of money a-
vailable versus costs of the job at this stage of the process
will help you decide where color can be used, whether the
format you desire is at all feasible, the quantities you can
print, and so on. Time spent comparing paper prices, costs
of bindery operations that might be avoided by a slight change
in format, how to get the color you want on one side of the
sheet instead of both, thereby saving one press run, will

be repaid many-fold later, when the job proceeds without backtracking and wheelspinning.

4. Determine the equipment available for the job. This is really a part of budget considerations, but knowing what equipment you have to work with will affect to some extent the way you proceed in planning your format and making layouts. This knowledge allows you to foresee restrictions. For example it is much harder to print large areas of solid color on a Multilith than on a large offset press, and you can avoid that kind of problem in making your plans.

5. Prepare rough sketches of your ideas for the job. These sketches are called "thumbnails" and are helpful for all but the smallest jobs. They are essential for complicated work. Remember in doing thumbnail sketches that the proportions of the final job must be maintained, or the thumbnail will give you a false sense of space and a line that appears to fit in the sketch won't fit in the final job. An easy way to keep proportion in the sketches is to fold a sheet of paper the size of the job into four quarters. Each quarter section is proportionately half the size of the job. You can try four versions of the layout in the four sections, measure the lines in the one you like, double them and you have all the sizes for the job. In sketching thumbnails, headings, pictures, and drawings try to establish a feeling of the weight and color they will have when printed. Large areas of copy should show margins accurately. You are trying to get a sense of balance with the proportions of heavy title and illustration areas opposing the lighter areas of type and drawings. If the job is heavily illustrated, thumbnails of each two-page spread should be drawn to assure that the balance and progression is smooth throughout. If the job is small and not filled with illustrations, a sketch of a typical page including as many elements as possible will serve. If the job is a single page broadside you can well afford to spend time on careful and elaborate sketches, as you have far less to work with and the placement of the elements has to be just right.

6. Make tracings of the more important parts of the job, such as covers and title pages of pamphlets, front panels of leaflets, entire broadsides. Tracings are used much more in book designing, where the typesetter and printer use them to go by in setting the book, and you may find that thumbnails are enough, especially if you don't have a customer to please. Your transfer type sheets are ready-made type specimens. Set up a complete alphabet of the types you are planning to use for headings on a separate sheet, and do your tracing from it. Try to maintain a feeling of the shape and weight of the letters, and imitate any color you may be using with colored pencils. Text areas should be ruled to show the exact number of lines that will appear. A page of text under the tracing paper will act as a guide. The most accurate effect of text lines is gained by drawing the tops and bottoms of the x-height (the height of a lower case letter).

7. After you have determined the format of your job, figure out how many lines in the column width you have chosen the manuscript will make. This is called *copy fitting* (or casting off--terms borrowed from bookmaking) and is not used as much by T square pushers, who seem to prefer to cut and shift and squeeze to make things fit. But it can be of tremendous help to know before you start typing the approximate length of the job, especially if it's a long one.

Essentially what you do when you fit or "cast copy" is to determine the number of characters in the manuscript. Then establish the number of characters per pica (1/6 inch) in the type face you are using. This information is either available in typesetters' specimens or can be determined by counting the average number of characters there are in ten picas of an average printed page, including capitals. If you average, say, 27 characters per 10 picas, the number of characters per pica is 2.7. If the lines you are setting are 20 picas wide, each line will set 540 characters. By dividing 540 into the total number of characters in your manuscript you arrive at the number of lines in the finished job.

To determine the number of characters in your manuscript you don't need to count each letter. Since standard typewriters have either 10 characters per inch (Pica type-- don't confuse with the unit of measure called a pica) or 12 characters per inch (Elite type), you have only to determine the average length of line in the manuscript. If the average line is 6 1/2 inches and the type is Pica, the number of characters per line is 65 (if Elite, 78). Count the number of lines in the manuscript and multiply by the number of characters per line, and you have the total number of characters in the manuscript. You should try to average short lines by grouping them with other short lines to equal a full line.

A device called the Haberule Copy Caster provides a scale with clear instructions for copyfitting most typefaces set by linotype, monotype, and phototypesetting techniques. If you are in a position to have type set professionally I recommend you use that. It sells for about $13.00.

Now the only problem is to relate the method I have just talked about to the IBM Executive. Since in most cases you will be typing unjustified lines the averages are going to be much rougher, because lines won't necessarily break right at the margin as they do with justified type. Even so, you should be able to treat the IBM in pretty much the same way you would type. Figure the average number of characters per pica (if you are using all inch measurements, which is probably easier if you don't work with hot type at all, just figure the average number of characters per inch) and multiply by the average length of line, which you can establish by typing out a few and measuring each one. If your typewriter averages 13 characters per inch and the average line is 2 3/4 inches, the number of characters per line when printed would be about 35. Then just treat the copy fitting as you would for hot type.

After you have cast the copy you should be able to combine the page it makes with the space that will be taken by headings and illustrations and see how it fits into the space you have. Then you will know if you need drastic rewriting or a whole new format. None of this is going to be sublimely accurate, but you will be close enough that you won't be unpleasantly surprised after the type is all set.

Talking to Printers

If you have followed the Seven Steps to Printerly Wisdom you are ready to Talk to Printers. I include this little section because a great deal of time seems to be wasted in miscommunications between printers and their clients. And since many readers will be using this book to help them get their printing done more easily and save some money while using the services of professionals, fostering greater ease in getting the work done helps all concerned.

If you have followed the steps above, you have already done most of what you need to do to be effective when proposing a job to your printer. If you can take to him a rough dummy of the job as you envision it he will be much better able to visualize in terms of camera and press, etc., the things you are talking about. Say you want to print a leaflet 8 1/2 x 11 inches, folded in thirds, on white paper, and in two colors. Take a sheet of paper, fold it in thirds, and scribble in the two colors where you think you want them. Already you have saved a lot of question-and-answer time. If you also know the quantities you are planning to print, and know that you are delivering camera-ready copy, then you have about all the information the printer needs in order to tell you whether or not he can do the job, what it will cost, and the problems that may be involved. The more complicated the job the more thinking and planning you should do in advance of talking to your printer. The Seven Rules should give you all you need for that.

The next step in talking to printers is Listening. I recently was asked to produce 25,000 envelopes of a size and shape that was out of the ordinary. The idea was a good one, but a quick call to an envelope maker revealed that an oddball

envelope costs almost twice as much to make as a standard
one. The budget just couldn't take it, but by shuffling a-
round samples of standard envelopes we were able to maintain the sense of the original design without spending the
extra money. If you have chosen a nice paper from your
sample book, your printer is the one to tell you it has to be
shipped from upstate New York and is only available in
2000 pound lots.

Give your printer time. Much of the above implies that
printers are wise old gents who should be treated with great
deference and respect, and they are. But I know all too well
that a lot of printers treat time in a vague, organic way,
truly believing that the time to start work on a job is when
the customer calls asking why it isn't ready. This attitude
probably comes from all the busy customers who constantly demand that their work is the most important and that
it must be done within a few hours. You will undoubtedly
see in some print shops the old cartoon in which the client
says to the printer: "Of course I want it today. If I'd wanted it tomorrow I'd have ordered it tomorrow." After a few
years of that printers start to get a little philosophical, and
the best way to get what you want when you want it is to allow for time on your side of the job, not on the printer's.
I don't expect you to believe any of this, but then I've become a little philosophical.

So far I have been talking about printers with whom you
develop an ongoing relationship, working within his scope
and limitations and making your own work fit the work your
printer can do. But there are situations that don't allow this
kind of relationship, for example a one-time printing job
that has to be done as cheaply as possible, when listening
to some garrulous printer is not part of the agenda. For
these readers I have performed an experiment with a near-
by "Instant Printing" franchise shop with an Itek and an
A. B. Dick duplicator. I designed and pasted up a twelve
page pamphlet of poems, with the typewriter used for this
book, and transfer type for the title page and the titles of

the poems. I pasted up the work on 8 1/2 x 11 inch paste-up sheets, to be reproduced at the same size and printed in black only. They were designed to be folded in half and inserted making a pamphlet 5 1/2 x 8 1/2 inches. One drawing was included, on the cover. I knew that to specify a paper would throw the printer into a frenzy, so I asked for his standard white paper. Nothing was said about binding, as I planned to do that myself, and the only requirement the printer had to follow was to back up the sheets as indicated by a dummy that I had provided. I ordered 100 copies at $7.50 per hundred per sheet for printing on two sides, or $28.50 for the whole job, including the cover.

Here are the results. There was nothing wrong with the actual printing of the job, if you don't count the generally gray, washed-out color of the ink. The position of the text as a whole on the printed sheets followed my layout fairly accurately, though there was obviously no attempt made to line up the two sides of the sheets with one another. The paper was as dull as could be feared; a plain cheap white bond of the kind used for sending poison pen letters and ransom notes. Asking for the sheets to be backed up according to a plan seemed to be as far as the shop could extend its creative facilities, and I might as well have been displaying a meteorite as a dummy for all the familiarity that was exhibited.

In general I would say these shops are great for flyers and the simplest of leaflets. In the shop I went to it costs $10.70 for one thousand copies, one side, one color, and 8 1/2 x 11 inch paper included. The unit cost decreases the more copies of any one thing you order. But avoid them for complex work, such as pamphlets or work involving color. They usually serve offices with quick duplicating needs, so my complaint that they aren't really printers is probably not completely justified. I just object to their making printing a simplistic word with the result that many people now believe that all printing is no better than the uninspired junk these shops produce.

Laying Out a Pamphlet

I am appending to this chapter a quick plan of how to lay
out a pamphlet, since I have not included it anywhere else,
and I just talked about preparing one for the printer. It
really is not anything difficult. All you have to remember
is that since the sheets will be folded and inserted inside
one another, the four pages that a sheet of paper includes
when it becomes part of the pamphlet are not necessarily
consecutive pages. Take for example the twelve page pamphlet I had printed instantly. There were three sheets of
paper, printed on both sides. The first sheet was printed
with pages 1 and 12 on one side, with 2 and 11 on the other.
The second sheet contained pages 3 and 10, while pages 4
and 9 backed it up. The middle sheet had pages 5 and 8
backed by 6 and 7. The way to make a pamphlet dummy,
no matter what the number of pages, is to fold the proper
number of sheets (three sheets for a twelve page pamphlet,
four sheets for sixteen, and so on) and number them. Taking
the dummy apart will show you which pages should be pasted up and printed with which others. This becomes more
complicated if you are using more than one fold in making
your pamphlet, and you should check with your bindery for
folding instructions. The illustration shows how an eight
page pamphlet would be made by printing on both sides of
a sheet and then folding as you would a French fold announcement mentioned in Chapter 8.

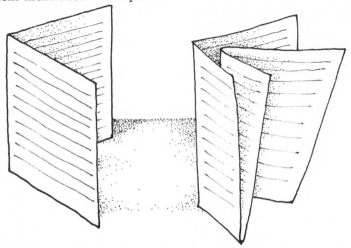

10 | Starting a Shop

So far in our discussion I have talked primarily as if the camera-ready copy were to be printed professionally, since the concern of this book is the design and preparation of copy rather than the technical aspects of printing. Also, camera and press work require training, which means the acquisition of experience that can't be gained from a book. However, that certainly doesn't preclude someone's buying a press and learning to print. There are already technical manuals available that deal with printing and camera processes. I have listed a couple in the bibliography, and browsing around will certainly unearth more.

But what if you have some experience, are willing to gain more, and see the creation of your own print shop as a way to work at something you like to do and a way to overcome the economic barriers to printing what you want? One used equipment dealer here in San Francisco says he gets a lot of people asking, "How do I get started? What do I need?" Individual needs and abilities vary so much that a specific list of requirements is impossible, but perhaps I can lay out a picture of what you'll be up against so you won't hope too high or despair too deep.

Aside from the paste-up studio, you need three basic pieces of equipment in your shop: a camera, a platemaker, and a press. You also need various work surfaces, for developing plates, etc., and a light table for stripping negatives, which we've discussed.

When you think of a print shop you naturally think of the press, and the tendency is to start a shop with that piece of equipment. But my experience has been that the really important and challenging work takes place at the camera stage--that's where you do the tricks and make the errors. If I were setting up a shop I would establish a camera and darkroom first, supplying a trade printer with negatives or plates, then go about finding a press. Of course your budget, circumstances, and experience may restrict you to getting the press.

Camera

While a press is a certain piece of equipment that you either have or don't have, a camera can be just about anything that will take a picture, from a homemade camera  built out of plywood for a few hundred dollars to a large $5000.00 graphic arts camera. You will probably find yourself somewhere in between depending on your finances, your experience, and your skill with tools. I talked to two San Francisco printers who have built their own cameras, Bob Meyer and Bob Hill, and they both recommend that, unless you are trained in wood or metal working, you expend your energies in getting the money for a professionally made camera rather than trying to build it yourself. Aside from being printers, Meyer is a skilled machinist and Hill is an expert woodworker and had worked as a professional cameraman.

There is no reason to suppose you are not entering the world of print after training as an engineer, so I have added a list of problems that are specific to cameras, things you should be aware of if you attempt to construct one.

1. The lens is all important. It is the one item you can't build and the better the lens the better the camera. Prices for lenses will range from $150.00 to $400.00 or $500.00.

2. The focal length of the lens in part determines the quality of the work you can get. Hill recommends a 19 inch focal length, which can be shot at f22. In theory the focal length should be as long as the diagonal of the largest work you are producing (or about 20 inches for an 11 x 17 inch negative) so this should be about right for a small camera. Hill uses an 18 inch lens and gets good results on film as large as 20 inches.

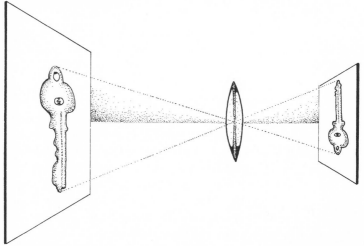

3. There are three plane surfaces in a camera that must be absolutely parallel in order to get proper work. The copy-board, the lens, and the back, or negative board, must all be in true alignment with each other. If not, part of the copy will be out of focus, or will be slightly larger or smaller at one point than the rest of the copy. This parallel must be maintained at all positions, for enlargements and reductions as well as same-size work. The illustration shows the relationship between the three elements.

4. Devise a system for focusing the camera from the back at the point where the negative will be exposed. This is best done as it is in commercial cameras: by the use of a ground glass in the back of the camera. Since two of the three elements in a camera must move in relationship to one another in order to enlarge and reduce copy, to maintain correct focus without the complex gear tracks of ready-made jobs you must be able to adjust focus each time you move the camera.

5. The light source must cast light evenly over the entire copyboard. Light that is brighter in one spot than another will result in a difference in exposure and in useless negatives. Hill uses four photofloods on fixed panels. Since his copyboard remains stationary the light source, when adjusted, is always correct. In cameras in which the copyboard moves to change reductions and enlargements, it is best to fix the lights to the copyboard in such a way that they move along with it; then the adjustments can be maintained.

6. The entire structure must be solid, so that jostling or the rumblings of machinery doesn't move the camera out of focus, thereby ruining the negative.

It will help immensely to read up on the theory of photography and cameras, and to look at professionally made cameras to discover ways of solving technical problems.

If you are buying a camera there are several things to keep in mind before you even consider brands and prices. First, remember that you will need a darkroom, darkroom equipment, and supplies. I will mention those things later, but for now, just remember that the price tag on the camera is not the end of your expenses. Second, consider the size of the work you will want to do, not the size you may be planning or doing at the moment, but the most realistic projection of where you are going as a printer. If you determine to make the most of a duplicator handling nothing larger than 11 x 17 inches, then a camera

that takes film 11 x 14 inches is all right for your purposes.
But if you secretly dream of large posters or big pamphlets
and books, you are wasting time and money setting up a camera and darkroom that will have to be entirely rebuilt later.
It's true that you can get lots of good experience on smaller equipment, and many of us have no idea where we might
be in a year or two. I'm just cautioning those who may think
a temporary solution is a good one. It ain't. The reason for
the tart words is that I am about to recommend a type of
camera to you that is restricted in size but which falls within a price range compatible with the costs of presses and
other small equipment you would need to set up a shop to
do the kind of work we have been talking about. A small
press is still useful for a myriad of purposes even after
you have a large one, but a small camera is just a nuisance
if you are trying to do large work. However, a small camera can be set up in a very restricted space, can be used
with a limited darkroom set-up, and at the same time can
provide you with top quality negatives, while giving you a
fair amount of latitude in the kinds of things you can do.

The field of small cameras is pretty diverse--more so
than I thought when I first started surveying it and I may
have missed something. Of course I wasn't buying; if you're
buying you'll find out pretty fast what's available. Basically,
prices on the new market range from just under $1000.00 to
about $1600.00 for cameras with a film capacity of 11 x 14
inches. Most small cameras are built vertically to save
space. The only true, small horizontal camera available is
the Argyle, a camera built just like the larger models, including a geared track for changing sizes, and quartz light-
ing. The closest I could get on a price for the Argyle was
$1200.00 to $1300.00, so you'd best check it out. This camera is made by a good firm and is pretty well respected. I
worked on one a few years ago, and although the boss had
it sitting on the floor in an empty bedroom, with the developing trays in a closet, it still did a good job.

One of the problems with a vertical camera is that when

you are reducing to a small size the copyboard is right down by the floor, which ultimately strains the back. And they are restricted in the reductions they can get because they don't have the range of a horizontal camera (in order to get very small reductions you would need a very tall vertical camera which no one could reach to work on). But the verticals save a tremendous amount of space, which is no doubt why most small cameras are built that way. If you are trying to compact your camera facility into a space that is already restricted, a horizontal would take too much floor space to be practical. But you can put a vertical camera into a very small darkroom. The cheapest vertical camera I have seen is the Sandmar, selling for $995.00; Agfa Gevaert makes one for about $1600.00. In between the two is the Goodkin at about $1200.00. You can see that costs are spread out; the real considerations are space limitations and personal preference.

In the used market all kinds of things can happen. Here you will find old copy cameras, ancient photographer's view cameras, busted cameras, broken cameras, and the like. One associate of mine got his large horizontal camera for $200.00; another found a big old copy camera for next to nothing and rebuilt it into a respectable graphics camera (he maintained, however, the old sliding film holder, and kept his darkroom in a closet). The smaller cameras seem to be selling for $500.00 to $1000.00 used, or about half of what they sell for new. You will find old junk cameras with good lenses that you can rebuild into something usable; or on the other hand, good camera bodies without lenses that you can get dirt cheap and buy good lenses for.

Darkroom equipment is as variable as the camera itself. For about $50.00 you can get a set of trays and a red safelight. You can build the safelight out of a box by taping a sheet of Rubylith over the open side, mounting a 40 or 60 watt bulb in one end and cutting holes in the other end for the heat to escape. That should cost you only a couple of dollars. While it is possible to spend several hundred dollars on a special sink, you can build one out of plywood and fiberglass resin--just a wooden tray with a drain, mounted on a table under the faucets. One of the best lithographers in San Francisco uses a set-up like that. To keep the developer at the right temperature, block off one part of your sink (or use a double drain) and float your developer tray on warm water, keeping a thermometer in the water at all times and adding hot or cold water to keep the temperature right. A handy device is a viewing frame made of frosted glass with lights behind it; they should be capable of being switched on and off independently from the other lights in the darkroom. If you are doing halftone work with a primitive setup like this you might want to mount red safelight bulbs in the frame as well as white ones, so you can examine the halftones as they are developing. All you really need for a darkroom is a room where you can mask off all light completely--either temporarily, or more preferably, permanently. Hot and cold running water is desirable though I have seen shops that do without. A bathroom, if at all large enough is ideal (it is where most hobby photographers put their darkrooms), or if you want to put your camera in the darkroom, perhaps a laundry room will do. Some friends of mine built a photography darkroom out of pieces of cardboard stapled to the studs of an unfinished basement. Remember that you need some kind of ventilation--those chemicals can really knock you out.

Platemaking

Platemaking equipment can just as easily be built at home as the equipment for your darkroom. All that you really need is a way of contacting your masked negatives to plates so that no air bubbles or any other gaps remain between the two while the plate is being exposed, and a light source that is strong enough to fully expose the plate in a reasonable amount of time. A contact frame can be built on a plywood base using any rubber sheet you can find that has waffling (bumps) on the surface. A 3M offset press blanket is perfect as the back side and has those patterns. You should be able to find a printer to give you an old one. Glue a strip of refrigerator sealing material around the blanket, and stick a valve like those used to repair tubeless tires through the blanket near one side. The valve is attached to a small vacuum pump, available for $50.00 or less. If a piece of glass is laid over this device, resting on the molding, and the pump is turned on, the blanket will be puffed up tightly against the glass, as the air between the glass and the blanket is pulled out by the pump. If an offset plate is placed on the blanket with a masked negative between it and the glass, the two will be contacted perfectly when the vacuum pump is in operation, and the mask (negative) being on the glass side exposes the right areas of the plate to the light source. The glass can be built into a window-type wooden frame, with the base frame and the glass frame hinged together to make a unit. Trunk hinges will pull the glass down against the base while the vacuum pump is being activated, so as to insure proper contact. This is a description not only of how to make a platemaker, but of how commercial platemakers are built.

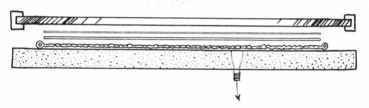

Your light source can be two or three strong photoflood lamps placed fairly close, ultraviolet light sources, or arc lamps. Arc lamps, which are used in commercial platemakers, are by far the best, but they are expensive. You will spend $100.00 to $200.00 for the most inexpensive nuArc models. I think they are worth the expense, if only because they cut exposure time considerably, which means time you don't spend standing around waiting for plates to burn. These arc lamps are free standing and you should find out from your supplier the proper distance from lamp to plate depending on what equipment and materials you are using.

There are platemakers especially designed for small offset duplicators, which use pressure to contact the masked negative and the plate, and these devices aren't worth a tinker's damn. They don't force all the air out between the negative and the plate, and you don't know they haven't done that until you develop the plate and find the big spot where the air bubble was. By then you have lost a 75 cent plate. With negatives containing windows and halftones they are impossible. The cheapest vacuum frame platemaker I have found is a nuArc model for just over $200.00. You can spend more than $1000.00 for a new platemaker, but by searching around you should be able to buy one used for under $100.00.

Press

Buying an offset press is like buying a used car--depending on where you find it you can pay widely varying prices for the same thing, and the more you know about the equipment the better your chances are of getting a good deal. Listed in the bibliography is a book called *Troubleshooter for 1250 Multi*, which will give you some pointers to help in choosing a press. Keep in mind that a set of rollers is very cheap for the small duplicators, so an otherwise sound press is a good buy even if the rollers are bad. The condition of the gears tells you more about the general condition of the press than anything, and of course you should insist on running it or seeing it run. I have always used cleanliness as a way of judging the condition of a press, but that is not always accurate, because a pressman can take good care of his machine without cleaning it. Of course, if you buy from a dealer the press may have been cleaned up even though it's in lousy shape. Finally, experience in running duplicators is the best training for picking one.

Since a new press is virtually out of the reach of my readers, I will only say that for any new 15 inch press you will pay upwards of $4000.00; a couple approach $5000.00. So,

being realistic I will run down the available used presses
with some of the costs.

Let me insert a quick note about used equipment dealers.
I have had my complaints about the prices they charge for
some equipment, and I still believe they charge too much.
They take markups as high as 50% to 100% depending on the
dealer and on the equipment, and this could be considered
marked up over the actual value of the equipment. On the
other hand you must remember that the dealer is finding
the equipment and keeping it around his warehouse for you
to come and buy. In terms of presses you can get a much
better price by buying privately and of course you can see
the press running. From a dealer the higher price often
covers some rebuilding, and you can insist on some kind
of warranty. Equipment dealers have been of tremendous
help to me, giving information as much as anything else.
In listing prices I will use those from the dealers, since
they are easy to get. Keep in mind that you can get lower
prices by finding a press on your own, and that by being in
the right place at the right time you can often get extraor-
dinary deals. In looking for a press, patience is an asset,
and within reason you should have no trouble eventually finding the press you want at the right price.

MULTILITH: The most common offset duplicator, and the
one you will find most easily. The standard model is the
1250 and there is a 1250W with slightly oversize cylinders
for handling 11 x 17 inch sheets. There have been three basic changes in the Multilith over the years, which are noted
by the color of the press. The black models are the earli-
est, and the browns followed. The current gray Multi was
released twelve to fourteen years ago. The color is a good
guide to the age of the press, and you can further check the
age by getting the serial number from the right hand casting at the delivery end of the press and calling Addresso-
graph-Multigraph. They keep a chart of the dates of all
serial numbers. Gray Multis are currently selling for about

$1000.00 from equipment dealers. Older gray models and brown models go for around $750.00 and may go for as little as $500.00.

A. B. DICK: As far as I know the A. B. Dick is the most expensive duplicator on the market, whether new or used. The main reason A. B. Dick presses are expensive is that they haven't been around long enough to get very old (they were first issued in 1957). The 350 model is a standard 10 x 15 inch maximum, and there is a 360 that will run an 11 x 17 inch sheet. A used 360 now sells for $1500.00 to $2000.00 on the average, though I'm sure there are cheaper ones around. There are a couple of advantages to A. B. Dick machines, which recommend them to those with the money to buy them. One is simple operation. Both models of the A. B. Dick machine use a system by which both water and ink run together on the same rollers. It is not necessary to learn as much about ink and water balances as with other duplicators. Also the A. B. Dick machines are very fast. I once ran one that was geared up to run close to 10,000 copies per hour.

CHIEF 15: This is my favorite press of the bunch. Built by American Type Founders, the Chief offset presses are extremely good machines in all the sizes. There is not a lot of difference between the Chief 15 and the Multi, though I find the Chief better built and generally more convenient to operate. Prices will range somewhere between the Multi and the A. B. Dick, although the Chiefs I have seen seemed high priced for used equipment.

HAMADASTAR: This is a recent Japanese entry, and I doubt if you'll find it on the used market yet. It's sort of a cross between the Multi and the Chief 15, borrowing a few features from each. It's very solidly built, and a friend who has run one says it's the best little press he's seen. Of course, in order to get one you have to have a lot to invest.

DAVIDSON: Here, at last, is a press you might find to let you into printing really cheaply. The old Davidson 221 is a 10 x 15 inch press built on a principle different from all the others--instead of three cylinders for plate, blanket and impression, the Davidson uses a large single cylinder for both the plate and impression. While the plate is being inked, the opposite side is impressing the sheet, upside down. This press is not only slower running, but it is slower to work on, because, instead of adjustable pressures between cylinders, the impression cylinder has to be packed manually for different thickness of paper, just as with large presses. But you should be able to find an old Davidson in running condition for $200.00 to $250.00. They're a very solid press, and if you're not battling the time pressures of commercial work, one of these could be perfect for you.

Paper Cutter

Finally you must consider the great paper cutter problem. In talking about paper I explained that you can have your supplier cut parent sheets down to the size you want to run. While it is an extra expense, it solves that immediate problem. The time a paper cutter becomes frightfully important is when you want to make a cut after the sheet has been run through the press, say for example when you run several of the same job, such as a small card, on the same sheet of paper to save press time, trimming bleed work to the right size and trimming pamphlets. It is possible to have a commercial bindery do this kind of cutting--more expense. Or you can find a munificent fellow printer to lend you time on his cutter--ultimately a nuisance to him and a lot of dashing about for you. Finally, as mentioned in Chapter 7, you can't make effective use of waste paper if you can't cut it yourself; if you have to pay to have it cut it loses its value as scrap.

If it is easy to agree that a cutter is desirable, it is harder to agree on the size and kind. The oldest hand-operated

cutters are still expensive, because cutters are always in demand and don't lose their value. So the tendency is toward buying a small one, just large enough to do your particular work. But this means that you still won't be able to cut large parent sheets, so a small cutter doesn't save you the money it should. You have to have a cutter at least 26 inches wide to handle 26 x 40 inch paper. (Any larger parent sheets usually come in a size half as large as well, or the supplier will make that single cut without charge.) An old hand-operated guillotine cutter can sell for as much as $600.00 or $700.00 from a dealer, but by scouring all the print shops in your area you may come up with one that has been replaced by a hydraulic cutter and that the owner is willing to sell to gain space. It is hard to get a cutter in bad condition since they are extremely well built. Make sure the backstop is solid, and that the blades are not hopelessly nicked or damaged. Even then, blades can be replaced.

There are scores of presses and cameras, hundreds of special circumstances that I have ignored in this survey, and it won't take you long to discover the particular problems you face in your own situation. Hopefully this clears up some murkiness and helps you to ask the right questions. **121**

The IBM Composer

As you advance in your work with the IBM Executive, you will learn how and when to use hot type techniques such as Linotype and Monotype. You will also discover the existence of more advanced (and expensive) cold type equipment. Typical examples are the Varityper and the Justowriter, and title-setting devices like the Headliner and the Strip-Printer. Except in specific instances the Varityper and the Justowriter are no better than the Executive, but there is one machine you should know something about.

The IBM Composer begins to look like the invention of the century for the underground designer and printer. It combines the capabilities of the Executive and the Selectric just as we were wishing for in Chapter 4. The size and style of type faces is changeable, and those faces are designed to look like type (at which the Exec makes only a passing effort). Not only that, but, although you still have to type the copy twice, the Composer has a gizmo that figures justification for you.

Why then, you say, didn't we just discuss the Composer and bypass all those gymnastics with the Exec. There are two reasons, one typographic and the other economic.

The Composer uses a unit system like that of the Exec, but instead of five units the Composer employs nine. Into those nine units the Composer fits faces ranging in size from six to twelve point, and in width from 1 to W. It's the old problem of limitations. You just can't accommodate that range of letters within such a limited width variation. What happens in the Composer is that in the small sizes all the letters are grotesquely wide, and in the large sizes the capitals are excessively narrow. Then into these limits they try to fit a traditional type face such as Baskerville or Bodoni and the result is a sham.

Where Composer faces are good, they are always in the ten to twelve point range, with eleven point being the best

size I found; the best styles are those designed most closely to fit the limitations of the machine. Adrian Frutiger
redesigned his Univers for the Composer. It is a face already proved sound and flexible in hot type applications,
and it remains the best in the Composer library. Journal
Roman, while an imitation of Times Roman, is good because it imitates a face that was designed for readability
under adverse conditions (newspapers).

The snare of the Composer is that, with the vast array
of type faces and sizes available, you think you have extensive typographic capability when you haven't. If you want
to do good work you are really restricted to two or three
types in one or two sizes. (It is better to reduce eleven
point type if you want it smaller, than it is to set it in a
small size to start with.)

The Composer costs $4400. 00, and rents for $180. 00 a
month. To rent one you must be able to pay three months
rent in advance and keep the machine at least six months
(or you lose the advance payment). The type balls, which
you must buy, cost $35. 00. I figure that to get into using
the Composer you would need $1500. 00 to invest. For that
price you could own two new Executives.

Don't despair at my negative attitude. The Composer is
definitely more flexible and typographically more sophisticated than the Exec. But we are dealing with limitations
as a creative force, and more ain't necessarily better.

Letterpress

I want to end this treatise on design for the small offset
with a note on letterpress printing. For certain people in
certain situations, a small letterpress hobby shop serves
the purpose better than a camera and offset press. There
are two things that might recommend this approach. First,
small letterpress equipment is much cheaper. Although
platen letterpresses have gone up in price lately, it is possible to find a good one for about $100. 00 (the going price

for a 10 x 15 inch hand-fed platen press, cleaned up by a dealer, is $350.00 and up). I know people who have paid as little as $10.00 for presses in working order, so these flukes do happen. For the rest of the equipment necessary you can browse the used equipment dealers, and watch for sales of equipment from shops going out of business. For $100.00 to $150.00 you ought to be able to acquire all the miscellaneous equipment you need. This includes: a type stand and type cases (an old open stand holding twelve cases should cost less than $50.00); a stone (a piece of marble on a small table will serve); a type stick for setting type; clippers for cutting spacing material; wooden "furniture" for filling the space around the type when printing; quoins and a quoin key for locking type into position for printing; strips of lead spacing material; racks for holding both furniture and spacing material. You can adapt the type stand to hold the stone, and use blank type cases to hold your spacing material and other miscellaneous items, thereby containing an entire shop within the space of a press and one cabinet. All you need beyond this is type and type spaces for word spacing and for the ends of short lines. For $100.00 you can get a minimum amount of spacing and type, roman and italic, in a single size. And for the price of a used IBM Exec you can get enough type to adequately handle small work. The best source for type and type information is MacKenzie and Harris, Inc., 659 Folsom Street, San Francisco 94107. Write for their catalog. For under $500.00, depending on what you pay for the press, you can be printing--an investment a third of that for offset equipment.

The second thing that recommends letterpress is the love of craft. If, as we have assumed previously, your intent is to get information out quickly and effectively, then a letterpress shop is not for you. While this in no ways implies that offset work need be hasty and slovenly, letterpress printing is a craft that asks minute attention to detail. Your time is spent in meticulously hand setting a broadside and getting perfect impression and color on the press.

Whatever approach you take, a knowledge and respect for the traditions of typography and printing will constantly improve and enliven your work. An electric typewriter can be as useful a typographic tool as handset type, a Multilith print as striking work as a letterpress only if both are seen as demanding crafts, capable and worthy of constant perfection.

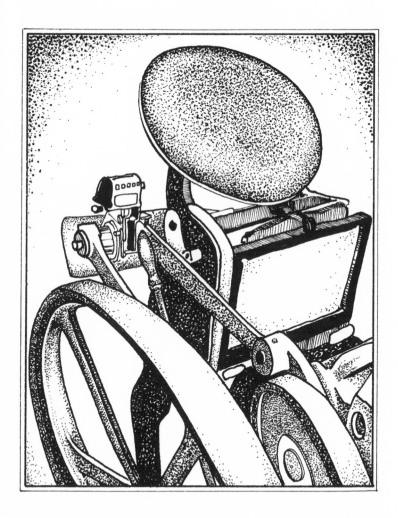

Bibliography

A. B. Dick Series on graphic design. Available through A. B. Dick sales outlets. Treats elementary design in terms of offset printing.

A Manual of Style; 12th Edition; University of Chicago Press, 1969. English style & usage, and fun to read.

Basic Bookbinding; A. W. Lewis; Dover Publications, Inc., New York, 1957. An excellent and inexpensive treatise on traditional bookbinding.

Bookmaking; Marshall Lee; Bowker, New York, 1965. You will never need all the information that's in this book.

Books and Printing; Paul A. Bennett, ed.; World Publishing Co., New York; Forum paper edition, 1963. A collection of essays on bookmaking and book collecting.

Creative Bookbinding; Pauline Johnson; University of Washington Press, Seattle, 1963, revised 1965. Better than the Lewis in that it is more to the purposes of this book, but expensive.

Essay on Typography; Eric Gill; J. M. Dent & Sons, London, 1960. I mentioned this book earlier. If you can't own it, at least read it.

Good Handwriting and How to Acquire It; John C. Tarr; J. M. Dent & Sons, London, 1965. Shows that calligraphy is not just an arty craft, but a useful everyday skill.

Kodak "Data Books." A vast source of information. Kodak issues publications on every area they make products for. Check with your Kodak supplier. The two data books on halftone reproduction are especially useful.

Lithographer 3 & 2; The Navy's manual on offset printing, and the best there is. Available from the Government Printing Office, P. O. Box 1533, Washington, D.C. 20013.

Papermaking; Dard Hunter; Alfred Knopf, New York, 1967. This book will teach you more about paper than you need to know. It's expensive, so get a copy from the library.

The Design of Books; Adrian Wilson; Reinhold/Studio Vista, New York, London, 1967. Buy this, even though it's expensive. You'll find yourself going back to it frequently to solve problems and get ideas.

The Puffin Book of Lettering; Tom Gourdie; Penguin Books, 1967. The best simple book on calligraphy.

Troubleshooter for 1250 Multi; Joseph Sellar; Reliable Duplicator Service, 75707 Sanford Sta., Los Angeles, Ca. 90005.

Webster's Collegiate Dictionary; any recent edition. This is the handiest dictionary to use at work: it's thorough but not too large to handle.

Writing and Illuminating and Lettering; Edward Johnston; Pitman, New York and Chicago, 1939. Another book that teaches far more than its subject.